Dial An Expert

The Consumer's Sourcebook of Free and Low-Cost Expertise Available by Phone

Dial An Expert

The Consumer's Sourcebook of Free and Low-Cost Expertise Available by Phone

• • •

Susan Osborn

• • •

A STONESONG PRESS/
PHILIP LIEF GROUP BOOK

McGRAW-HILL BOOK COMPANY

New York • *St. Louis* • *San Francisco*
Auckland • *Bogotá* • *Guatemala*
Hamburg • *Johannesburg* • *Lisbon* • *London*
Madrid • *Mexico* • *Montreal* • *New Delhi*
Panama • *Paris* • *San Juan* • *São Paulo*
Singapore • *Sydney* • *Tokyo* • *Toronto*

DIAL AN EXPERT

Created and developed by The Philip Lief Group, Inc. and The Stonesong Press, Inc.

First McGraw-Hill Paperback edition, 1986
1 2 3 4 5 6 7 8 9   FGRFGR   8 7 6

ISBN 0-07-019945-0

LIBRARY OF CONGRESS CATALOGING-IN-PUBLICATION DATA

Osborn, Susan.
  Dial an expert.

  "A Stonesong Press/Philip Lief Group book."
  1. Consultants—United States—Directories.
  2. Consumer education—United States—Directories.
I. Title.
HD69.C6083   1986   658.4'6'02573   85-24210
ISBN 0-07-019945-0

Book design by Beth Tondreau

Contents

Outdoors and Recreation 163
   General Information 163
   Boating Classes 164
   Boating Safety 164
   Conservation 165
   Mountaineering 165
   Ornithology 166
   See also Sports and Athletics

Parenting, *see* Pregnancy, Birthing, and Family Planning
   Adoption, *see* Children and Child Care: Adopting
      Special Children
   Lesbians, *see* Pregnancy, Birthing, and Family Planning:
      Lesbian Mothers
   Single, *see* Children and Child Care: Single Parents

Performing Arts 167
   General Information 167
   Theater 168

Personal Finances 168
   Banking 168
      See also Business: Banking
   Charities 169
   Collectibles, *see* Collectibles
   Commodities 170
   Credit, *see* Business: Credit Unions
   Family Economics 170
   Financial Planning 171
   Funeral Costs, *see* Death and Dying: Funeral
      Arrangements
   Futures and Options 172
   Income Taxes 172
   Insurance 172
   Investment Clubs 173
   Personal Property Appraisals 174
      See also Home Maintenance: Real Estate Appraisals
   Stocks 174
   U.S. Savings Bonds 176

Pet Care 177

Poison Control Centers 177

Postal Service 180
   Complaints 180

Introduction

The other morning, a friend of mine was pitting cherries for a pie. In his enthusiasm, some of the juice splashed onto his new Lacoste shirt (I swear the morsel was heading for his mouth, not the pie plate). "Isn't there anybody who can tell me how to get this out?" he hollered from the bathroom, as I blithely finished off the cherries.

It was the staff of the Stain Removal Hotline at the Philadelphia College of Textiles and Science (see Fabrics and Textiles: Stain Removal) who finally put him out of his misery. This organization is just one of the hundreds around the country that are willing, in fact, eager to provide consumers with free information over the phone. And *Dial An Expert* is a personal service directory that links consumers with hundreds of sources of immediate information, advice, counseling, and referrals. The people you will speak to are the experts on the staffs of university libraries and foundations; labor and business institutes; volunteer groups; municipal, state, and federal agencies; and hotlines. They work at alliances, centers, clubs, and just about every other kind of organization where people come together to promote or study some field or activity, and they are paid to put their knowledge at your disposal on queries ranging from the mundane to the esoteric—most for no more than the price of a phone call.

Although the choice of entries was selective (only organizations that have personnel trained to communicate information to consumers over the telephone are included), you'll find here an unparalleled variety of reliable and accessible sources of information. The directory is divided by general category. I've tried to provide enough information about each organization so that you can intelligently choose the service that will best satisfy your information needs. However, if you don't find the service that you need under a particular category, check related subject areas.

Each entry includes the following:

1. Information about the organization.
2. Information about the service offered (counseling, factual or how-to information, referrals, advice).
3. The hours in which calls are accepted.
4. The mailing address of the organization.
5. The telephone number of the organization followed by the states served by the numbers listed.

Basically, three different kinds of telephone numbers are included: Numbers prefixed by the area code 800 are toll-free. Numbers prefixed by 900 cost the caller 50 cents (regardless of the time you place your call or the duration of the call). An itemized listing of charges for dialing standard area codes can be found in the first few pages of your local phone directory.

○ How to Get the Most Out of *Dial An Expert*

- Always dial "1" before dialing a number not prefixed by the same area code as the number from which you are calling. This includes 800 and 900 numbers.
- In general, you'll save money by dialing during weekends (from 6 P.M. Friday to 5 P.M. Sunday) and after 6 P.M. on weekdays.
- When dialing an 800 number, remember that the organization you are calling has paid for the use of this service. These organizations request, therefore, that before dialing you have at hand all the information you think you'll need. When the staff member answers, be straightforward; explain exactly what you need. You may end up repeating yourself once or twice, but it does, in the long run, expedite your receipt of the information.
- If you call an organization after their business hours and get an answering machine, speak directly into the mouthpiece of your telephone and speak as clearly

as possible when you leave your message. Leave all the information you think the organization will need to return your call. If you suspect that the organization you're calling will have difficulty understanding your name and/or address, spell them out. If you're leaving your phone number, don't forget to include your area code; if leaving your address, don't forget your zip code. You might also, for your convenience and theirs, indicate the best time for you to receive a return call.

- Every attempt has been made to make *Dial An Expert* an up-to-date and accurate consumer directory. If by chance the number you dial has been changed since our publication date, you will most likely reach a tape announcing the correct number. If you don't, dial the appropriate area code and **555-1212** and ask the information operator for the new listing. If you get hold of the company but the extension of the person you're looking for has been changed, ask for the correct extension.

- If for any reason you cannot make any connection with the number you're trying to reach, call the operator and explain your difficulty. He or she will place the call for you, and you will be charged at the direct-dial rate. If you reach a wrong number, are confronted with a poor connection, or are cut off, hang up and dial the operator immediately. Explain what happened and the operator will arrange for you to receive the proper credit.

- Many of the organizations listed, especially those that use 800 numbers, are especially busy at certain times of the day. If you receive a repeated busy signal, try calling at a different time of the day. In general, I found that early morning (before 10:30 A.M. in the area I was calling) and late afternoon (after 3:30 P.M.) were the best times to call.

- If you use a telecommunications service for the deaf or other special communication device and need help placing your call, dial **800-555-1155**. An operator will assist you.

My thanks to all those who generously shared information and resources with me, especially Kathryn Meier at the Women's Health Network, Nora Coffey at HERS, Cheryle Gartley at the Simon Foundation, Kathleen Kelley at Closer Look, and Paul Fargis of the Stonesong Press. Special thanks to Philip Lief for his expert advice and counsel, among other things.

Dial An Expert

The Consumer's Sourcebook of
Free and Low-Cost Expertise
Available by Phone

A

• AERONAUTICS AND SPACE EXPLORATION

○ General Information

If you have a question about any aspect of aeronautics or space exploration, call the National Air and Space Museum Library. The librarian will fill you in on early aircraft, modern air technology, and the pioneers of flight. Without a doubt, this is the place to call for information about the right stuff. Telephone inquiries are handled every weekday between 10 A.M. and 4 P.M. eastern standard time (EST).

National Air and Space Museum Library
7th Street and Independence Avenue SW
Washington, DC 20560
202-357-3133

○ Mission and Flight Information

If you're wondering why the space shuttle that was supposed to go off at 10:00 this morning didn't, call one of the NASA facilities listed below. These four prerecorded messages give details of NASA programs as well as information on the purpose of various missions and on what's happening in space that day. The status reports are updated every weekday morning (more frequently during flights), and calls are answered 24 hours a day, every day of the week.

Goddard Space Flight Center
Greenbelt, MD
301-344-0890

Johnson Space Center
Houston, TX
713-483-6111

Marshall Space Flight Center
Huntsville, AL
205-453-2803

Kennedy Space Center
Kennedy Space Center, FL
305-867-2525

● **ALCOHOLISM** See *Business: Alcohol Rehabilitation Programs; Health: Alcoholism.*

● **APPLIANCES**

○ **Complaints** See *Consumer Complaint Services: General Complaints.*

○ **Product Information** See *Information Centers: Product Information.*

○ **Repairs** See *Home Maintenance: Appliance Repair.*

● **APPRAISALS**

○ **Art** See *Collectibles: Art Appraisals.*

○ **Jewelry** See *Collectibles: Jewelry Appraisals.*

○ **Personal Property** See *Personal Finances: Personal Property Appraisals.*

○ **Real Estate** See *Home Maintenance: Real Estate Appraisals.*

● **ASTRONOMY**

○ **General Information**

The Astronomy Hotline, sponsored by the Astronomical Society of the Pacific (ASP), one of the oldest astronomical organizations in the world, offers 3 minutes of prerecorded information on the latest discoveries and innovations in the world of celestial science. The information is conveyed in nontechnical language (the ASP considers itself a bridge between the research community and the public) and is updated once a week. The answering machine is prepared to answer your call 24 hours a day, every day of the year.

Astronomy Hotline
Astronomical Society of the Pacific
1290 24th Avenue
San Francisco, CA 94122
415-661-0500

○ Weekly Events

Is it a bird? Is it a plane? Is it . . . ? Call your nearest astronomy hotline and find out. Each of the five listed below will give you prerecorded information detailing the major astronomical events of the week and suggesting the best ways to view them. The tapes run from 1 to 3 minutes, and each is updated, generally speaking, once a week. The answering machines will take your call 24 hours a day, every day of the week.

"Dial-A-Phenomenon"
Smithsonian Institute
1000 Jefferson Drive SW
Washington, DC 20560
202-357-2000
This 3-minute tape is updated once a week, usually on Wednesdays.

"Earth and Space Report"
Smithsonian Astrophysical Observatory
60 Garden Street
Cambridge, MA 02138
617-491-1497
This 3-minute tape is updated once a week, usually on Wednesdays.

"SKYLINE"
Sky Publishing Corp.
49 Bay Street
Cambridge, MA 02238
617-497-4168
This 3-minute tape, which is updated at least once a week, will provide you with specific viewing information as well as details of current news from the astronomical world.

"Skywatchers Report"
Department of Astronomy
University of Texas
Austin, TX 78712
512-471-5007
This 2-minute tape is updated once a week, usually on Mondays, except during school vacations, when it may be updated only every two weeks.

"STAR-line"
Abrams Planetarium
Michigan State University
East Lansing, MI 48824
517-332-STAR
This 1-minute tape is updated roughly once a week, depending on school vacations.

● **ATHLETICS** See *Sports and Athletics.*

● **AUTOMOBILES**

○ **Children's Safety Restraints**

If you're wondering what to look for when you set out to buy a child's car restraint, call the National Child Passenger

Safety Association. Although the staff will not recommend a certain brand, they will provide enough details so that you will be able to make an informed decision. The association, which serves both the professional and lay communities, also makes available information on seat-belt use for children, state laws affecting drivers and children, and current research. Some general safety information is also available. A clearing-house staff member will answer your call any weekday between 9 A.M. and 5 P.M., EST.

National Child Passenger Safety Association
P.O. Box 65616
Washington, DC 20035–5616
202-429-0515

○ Purchasing Information

If the thought of negotiating the price of your new car makes you squeamish, call Car/Puter International, an automobile data base. For $20 plus 75 cents postage per model, they'll send you a computer printout listing the dealer's cost and list price for any basic foreign or domestic car and the prices of available factory-installed options. A work sheet for calculating the total cost of add-ons is included with the printout. Upon request, Car/Puter will also suggest a local dealer. If you phone in your request with a credit card number, the packet is mailed out the same day; have the precise make and model number on hand when you call. The line is open weekdays from 9 A.M. until 5 P.M., EST.

Car/Puter International Corporation
1603 Bushwick Avenue
Brooklyn, NY 11207
800-221-4001
718-455-2500 (In New York)

The *Consumer Reports* Auto Price Service also provides an excellent starting point from which to negotiate the price of a new car. It is particularly useful when comparing domestic models, which offer a large selection of options that are frequently discounted. In return for your call, you will receive a list price and dealer's cost for the make and model you're interested in as well as for available factory-installed options, a reprint of an article on how to negotiate the price of a car, and a recommendation for minimal equipment. Costs are $10 for one car, $18 for two, $25 for three, and $8 for each additional, payable by VISA or MasterCard. (No auto information will be given over the phone.) Call weekdays between 9 A.M. and 5 P.M., EST.

Consumer Reports Auto Price Service
P.O. Box 570
Lathrup Village, MI 48076
800-528-6050, ext. **2279**

o Repair

The staff at Loctite will offer advice on almost any home repair from sealing an oil pan to treating rust creeping along your metal siding, usually via a company product. "Choose 'n Use Fix-It" guides are available that offer information on repairing your house or car, again usually using a company product. Their service is not to be discounted though—Loctite has an enormous selection of chemicals and fillers from which to choose. A research chemist is on the line to answer your questions weekdays from 8 A.M. until 5 P.M., EST.

Loctite Hotline
Automotive and Consumer Group
445 Crawford Court
Cleveland, OH 44128
800-321-9188
216-475-3600 (In Ohio)

o Safety   (See also *Mobile Home Safety Standards.*)

The Auto Safety Hotline provides safety-related information on all makes and models of cars, both foreign and domestic, available in the United States. Although specific recommendations cannot be given, enough data is provided for informed comparisons. Answers may also be found regarding federal and state laws on road signs and drunken driving, and complaints may be filed regarding auto safety. Callers are requested to confine their queries to safety-related issues. A representative will talk with you weekdays from 8 A.M. to 4 P.M., EST; a taped message will greet you at other hours.

Auto Safety Hotline
National Highway Traffic Safety Administration
Department of Transportation
400 7th Street SW
Washington, DC 20590
800-424-9393
202-426-0123 (In Washington, DC)

Wondering how safe that sports coupe that you've got your eye on is? The experts at the Insurance Institute for Highway Safety will answer any questions you have regarding the crashworthiness of almost any model car. They will also supply you with the theft history of a car you're interested in purchasing and give you performance statistics about various car-related items such as children's car seats. The phone is answered weekdays between 9 A.M. and 5 P.M., EST.

Insurance Institute for Highway Safety
Communications Department
Watergate 600 NW
Washington, DC 20037
202-333-0770

○ Tires

The Tire Industry Safety Council—an association of U.S. tire manufacturers—offers information to consumers about all aspects of tire care and safety. If you're wondering about the proper tire size for your car, the staff at the council will advise you; if you're wondering about the proper inflation pressure for your tires, they'll tell you about that also. The staff member I spoke to assured me that he could even diagnose the reason for my rear tire's uneven tread (his diagnosis was borne out by my mechanic). A tire expert will answer your call any weekday between 9 A.M. and 5 P.M., EST.

Tire Industry Safety Council
844 National Press Building
Washington, DC 20045
202-783-1022

B

● **BANKING**

○ **Commercial** See *Personal Finances: Banking.*

○ **Personal** See *Personal Finances: Banking.*

● **BATTERED WOMEN** See *Domestic Violence Hotlines.*

● **BIRTHING** See *Pregnancy, Birthing, and Family Planning.*

● **BOOKS** See *Reading and Writing: Book Search; Reading and Writing: Books for the Blind and Physically Handicapped.*

● **BUSINESS**

○ **Accommodating the Handicapped**

Mainstream, Inc., was founded in 1975 to prepare employers for recruiting and hiring qualified disabled people. Mainstream has designed affirmative action plans, developed in-house attitude and awareness training programs, and evaluated recruiting sources nationwide. When you call, an information specialist will seek out an answer or will send you an information packet, as needed. Disabled consumers are also encouraged to call for tips on résumé writing, the job search, and the job interview. Referrals to legal sources are also available. Call any weekday between 9 A.M. and 5 P.M., EST.

Mainstream, Inc.
1200 15th Street NW
Washington, DC 20005
202-833-1136

The experts at the Job Accommodation Network will provide business owners, school superintendents, government officials, and any other interested people with ideas for accommodating handicapped people in the workplace. The phone is answered on weekdays from 8 A.M. until 8 P.M., EST.

Job Accommodation Network
P.O. Box 468
Morgantown, WV 26505
800-526-7234
304-293-7186 (In West Virginia)

O Alcohol Rehabilitation Programs

Employee assistance programs (EAPs) are primarily designed to help all employees and their families who are alcohol abusers or affected by the disease of alcoholism. In addition to treating alcoholism, most programs offer assistance in other areas, such as drug dependencies and marital, legal, interpersonal, and occupational problems. For more information on occupational alcoholism programs, call the number listed below any weekday between 9 A.M. and 5 P.M., EST.

Association of Labor-Management
  Administrators and Consultants on
  Alcoholism, Inc.
1800 N. Kent Street
Suite 907
Arlington, VA 22209
703-522-6272

O Banking

The National Association of Bank Women (NABW) is the largest organization of financial executives in the world (its membership is over 30,000), and although it is the only one devoted specifically to the professional interests and advancement of women in the financial services industry, it welcomes calls from anyone involved or interested in banking. Beverly Firestone, director of research, can provide callers with a wide range of topical information on educational programs at all stages of career development, including senior-level training, management skills, and public affairs. She can also provide statistics, culled from NABW's wide variety of publications, research surveys, and special reports, on working women, women and banking, and trends and future direction of the industry. Firestone will also provide entrepreneurs and consumers with information on what to look for in a bank and how to approach a loan officer. Calls are accepted every weekday between 8:45 A.M. and 4:45 P.M. central standard time (CST).

National Association of Bank Women
500 N. Michigan Avenue
Chicago, IL 60611
312-661-1700

The American Bankers Association's "Washington Wire," a prerecorded message, offers details of legislative and regulatory news affecting bankers and the banking industry. The message is changed daily, and calls are answered 24 hours a day.

"Washington Wire"
American Bankers Association
1120 Connecticut Avenue NW
Washington, DC 20036
800-424-2871
202-467-5288 (In Washington, DC)

O Career Education   See *Education: Educational Resources; Job Counseling.*

O **Consumer Relations** See *Consumer Complaint Services: General Complaints and Inquiries.*

O **Copyright Information** See *Reading and Writing: Copyright Information.*

O **Credit Unions**

More and more small business owners are realizing that they can boost fringe benefits for their employees by affiliating with an existing credit union or by starting a new one. If you're interested in finding out more about federally insured credit unions—what they are, how to find one, how to organize one—call the National Credit Union Administration regional office that serves your area.

Region 1 (CT, ME, MA, NH, NJ, NY, PR, RI, VT, VI)
441 Stuart Street
Sixth Floor
Boston, MA 02116
617-223-6807
Weekdays, 8 A.M. to 5 P.M., EST

Region 2 (DE, DC, MD, PA, VA, WV)
1776 G Street NW
Washington, DC 20006
202-682-1900
Weekdays, 8:30 A.M. to 5 P.M., EST

Region 3 (AL, AR, FL, GA, KY, LA, MS, NC, SC, TN)
1365 Peachtree Street NE
Suite 540
Atlanta, GA 30367
404-881-3127
Weekdays, 8 A.M. to 4:30 P.M., EST

Region 4 (IL, IN, IA, MI, MN, MO, OH, WI)
230 South Dearborn
Suite 3346
Chicago, IL 60604
312-886-9697
Weekdays, 7:30 A.M. to 4:30 P.M., CST

Region 5 (AZ, KS, NV, NM, OK, TX, UT)
611 East Sixth Street
Suite 407
Austin, TX 78701
512-482-5131
Weekdays, 7:30 A.M. to 5 P.M., CST

Region 5 (suboffice) (CO, ID, MT, NE, ND, SD, WY)
10455 E. 25th Avenue
Suite 203
Aurora, CO 80010
303-844-3795
Weekdays, 7:30 A.M. to 4:30 P.M., MST

Region 6 (AK, American
Samoa, CA, Guam, HI, OR,
WA)
2890 N. Main Street
Suite 101
Walnut Creek, CA 94596
415-486-3490
Weekdays, 8 A.M. to 4:30
    P.M., PST

○ Developing Career and Family Options (See also *Job Counseling: Displaced Homemakers.*)

Catalyst is a national not-for-profit organization that works
with corporations and individuals to develop career and family options. Currently, Catalyst's principal programs include
the Career and Family Program (assists companies in formu-
lating policies that enable employees to successfully combine
work and family responsibilities; areas of interest include child
care, maternity and paternity leave, and alternative work
schedules); a Relocation Resource (helps employers meet the
special needs of two-career couples); the Benefits Program
(helps companies establish cost-effective flexible benefits plans
that meet the needs of the changing work force); the Upward
Mobility Program (analyzes barriers to women's advancement); the Corporate Board Resource (conducts searches for
high-level women eligible for directorship positions); Campus
Resource (raises students' awareness of career and personal-
life options); the Library and Audiovisual Center (a resource
of information about career and family issues); and the National Network of Career Resource Centers (a listing of qualified career and educational counseling centers around the
country). If you would like more information about any of
these programs, call Monday through Thursday from 9 A.M.
to 7:30 P.M. and on Fridays from 9 A.M. to 5 P.M., EST.

Catalyst
250 Park Avenue South
New York, NY 10003
212-777-8900

O Establishing a Smoke-Free Workplace See *Civil Rights: Nonsmokers' Rights; Health: Smoking.*

O Exporting

If you're wondering how to get the needed capital to market and produce goods or services for export, the Export/Import Bank, a government agency charged with facilitating U.S. exports through export finance programs, may be able to help. The bank hotline will give you information on four programs especially designed for those who are new to exporting and for small and medium-sized businesses. It will also direct you to further sources of assistance. The hotline is answered on weekdays from 9 A.M. to 5 P.M., EST.

Business Advisory Hotline
Export/Import Bank of the United States
811 Vermont Avenue NW
Washington, DC 20571
800-424-5201

If you're interested in exporting your product and you need some information on product standards and certification in foreign countries, call the Product Standards Policy office of the National Bureau of Standards. The staff will provide you with information on international and national technical regulations regarding product standards; calls are answered every weekday between 8:30 A.M. and 5 P.M., EST.

National Bureau of Standards
Product Standards Policy
Administration Building
Room A629
Gaithersburg, MD 20899
202-921-3751

For less personalized, more general information, call **202-921-3200** during the same hours. The prerecorded message offers information on selected international trade regulation matters from the General Agreement on Tariffs and Trade (GATT) secretariat in Switzerland.

o Federal Assistance

The Office of Business Liaison of the U.S. Department of Commerce offers callers information, advice, and guidance on various federal policies and programs of interest to businesspeople, including details on selling to government markets and financial assistance programs. Certain domestic and international business statistics are also available from this office. Call any weekday between 8:30 A.M. and 5 P.M., EST.

Office of Business Liaison
U.S. Department of Commerce
Room 5898C
Washington, DC 20230
202-377-3176

o Franchise Information

If you're interested in buying a franchise but feel on slightly shaky ground, the International Franchise Association is the place to go for advice. They will supply you with information on how to evaluate a franchise opportunity from every angle; they will also provide you with a list of association members that details, for each, the type of business, the history of the business, the cash needed for the business, and the qualifications for potential franchisees. The phones are answered weekdays from 8:30 A.M. to 5 P.M., EST.

International Franchise Association
1350 New York Avenue
Suite 900
Washington, DC 20008
202-628-8000

O Insurance (See also *Personal Finances: Insurance.*)

If you want information on low-cost federal crime and flood insurance, call the number listed below. The office is open every weekday from 9 A.M. to 5 P.M., EST.

Federal Insurance Administration
Federal Management Agency
500 C Street SW
Washington, DC 20472

Flood insurance:
800-638-6620
202-731-5300 (In Washington, DC, area or if
you have trouble reaching the 800 number)

Crime insurance:
800-638-8780
301-652-2637 (In Washington, DC, area or if
you have trouble reaching the 800 number)

O Marketing Information

Taxpayers pay the U.S. International Trade Commission thousands of dollars each year to investigate various commodities. These studies, many of which compare the volume of imports to domestic production and consumption, are available to all citizens and can be particularly helpful to businesspeople looking for new markets or for opportunities in old markets. In the past, the ITC has studied, among other things, ice hockey sticks, clothespins, and paper clips. If you want to know if a commodity that you're interested in has been investigated, call the publications clerk. If you know a report has been done and want to order a copy of the study, leave a message on the ITC's "Dial-A-Publication" number. The study will be mailed to you. Both offices are open every weekday between 9 A.M. and 5 P.M., EST.

U.S. International Trade Commission
701 E Street NW
Washington, DC 20436
Publications clerk: **202-523-0036**
"Dial-A-Publication": **202-523-5178**

o **Occupational Safety** See *Health: Occupational Safety.*

o **Patents and Trademarks**

If you need information on filing for a patent or trademark, call the number listed below. Calls are answered weekdays between 8:30 A.M. and 5 P.M., EST.

Commissioner of Patents and Trademarks
P.O. Box 9
Washington, DC 20231
202-557-3428

o **Services for Women** (See also *Information Centers: Women.*)

The American Woman's Economic Development Corporation (AWED) is a nationwide nonprofit organization that offers telephone counseling for women on every aspect of business growth, development, and management—whether you offer a product or a service and whether your business is in the earliest planning stage or already established. Appointments for long telephone conferences are available and can be set up when you call. The fee for a long conference is $25 payable by credit card or check. The phone is answered weekdays, 9 A.M. to 5 P.M., EST.

American Woman's Economic
    Development Corporation (AWED)
The Lincoln Building
60 E. 42 Street
New York, NY 10165
800-222-AWED
800-422-AWED (In New York)
212-692-9100 (In New York City)

The Federation of Organizations for Professional Women (FOPW) is a national nonprofit federation of affiliated organizations joined together to enhance the professional status of women, to impact public policy about professional women, and to exchange ideas and information. Because FOPW is a networking organization, the staff can provide you with information on almost any aspect of professional women's affairs, including discrimination problems, employment opportunities, and grant information. Contacts and referrals are also provided. Their national directory, *A Woman's Yellow Book*, provides a comprehensive and up-to-date listing of organizations concerned with women's issues; it is available to individuals for $12 and to schools, businesses, and libraries for $15. For more information call any weekday between 9 A.M. and 5 P.M., EST.

Federation of Organizations for
  Professional Women
1825 Connecticut Avenue NW
Suite 403
Washington, DC 20009
202-328-1415

○ Sexual Harassment

The Working Women's Institute (WWI) is a national research, training, and consultation center. The institute's focus is on equal employment opportunities for women and, specifically, the impact of sexual harassment and gender bias on working women. The institute staff can assist you in the following ways. First, they can design research on the issue of sexual harassment and gender bias in your organization. The findings from these studies can be applied to your situation to assess your specific needs. Second, WWI can help you design programs to address sexual harassment or take preventive measures within your organization. WWI conducts approximately 100 workshops each year—ask for information when you call. The office is open weekdays from 1 P.M. to 5 P.M., EST.

Working Women's Institute
593 Park Avenue
New York, NY 10021
212-838-4420

o Small Businesses

The Small Business Administration, a government-sponsored organization, is the first place inexperienced entrepreneurs should turn to for information about starting or running a small business. The trained staff will provide you with suggestions about setting up shop and give you information about training courses available in your area, sources of financial assistance, and special programs for women and veterans. The SBA also provides financial and management assistance to small businesses and offers loans to victims of floods, natural disasters, and other catastrophes. Call weekdays between 9 A.M. and 5 P.M., EST.

Small Business Administration
1441 L Street NW
Washington, DC 20416
800-368-5855
202-653-7561 (In Washington, DC)

C

• **CHARITIES** See *Personal Finances: Charities.*

• **CHILDREN AND CHILD CARE** (See also *Health: Maternal and Child Health; Pregnancy, Birthing, and Family Planning.*)

○ **Abuse**

The trained professionals who operate this hotline will provide both parents and children with information and counseling on child abuse—be it physical, sexual, or emotional. They will also carry out limited research for scholars interested in child abuse. Referrals to counseling centers are available, as are publications in English and Spanish on prevention programs and treatment. The phone is answered 24 hours a day, every day of the year.

National Child Abuse Hotline
Child Help U.S.A.
Woodland Hills, CA 91370
800-422-4453

The staff at the Parents Anonymous Hotline will provide you with information on self-help groups for parents involved in child abuse and for parents who fear becoming involved in child abuse. Crisis counselors are available when needed. The staff will refer you to another counseling center if it turns out that abuse is not the problem. The line is open 24 hours a day, year round.

Parents Anonymous Hotline
22330 Hawthorne Boulevard
Suite 210
Torrance, CA 90505
800-421-0353
800-352-0386 (In California)

o Adopting Special Children

The primary goal of the organization listed below is to aid potential adoptive parents of children with special needs. Through their adoption exchange, they match families with appropriate children and provide referrals to support groups who can provide encouragement and lay advice. A staff member will field your inquiries any weekday between 8:30 A.M. and 5 P.M., PST.

Aid to Adoption of Special Kids
P.O. Box 11212
Oakland, CA 94611
415-451-1748

o Auto Safety See *Automobiles: Children's Safety Restraints.*

o Bereaved Parents and Siblings

Parents of Murdered Children, Inc., is a self-help organization that provides ongoing emotional support for families cruelly bereaved. They will write or phone any parent of a murdered child and, if possible, link that parent up with others in the same vicinity who have survived their child's homicide. Referrals to local chapters are also made. The staff is willing to work with any professional in the field of law, mental health, social work, medicine, education, religion, and mortuary science who is interested in learning more about survivors of homicide. Call any weekday from 9 A.M. to 5 P.M., EST.

Parents of Murdered Children, Inc.
1739 Bella Vista
Cincinnati, OH 45237
513-721-LOVE
After 5 P.M., dial **513-242-8025;** your message will be recorded and your call returned as soon as possible.

The Compassionate Friends, Inc., is a voluntary, self-help group that tries to help all bereaved parents through mutual friendship and understanding. The group works to foster the physical and emotional health of bereaved parents and siblings through positive resolution of the grief experienced on the death of a child. There are 460 chapters across the country; the Illinois office listed below will refer you to the one nearest you. Publications and tapes are also available. Call weekdays between 9 A.M. and 4 P.M., CST.

The Compassionate Friends, Inc.
P.O. Box 3696
Oak Brook, IL 60522–3696
312-323-5010

○ **Birth Defects** See *Health: Spina Bifida; Pregnancy, Birthing, and Family Planning: Toxic Substances and Birth Defects.*

○ **Breast-Feeding**

If you're having trouble breast-feeding, call the La Leche League. Staff members will provide you with information about coping strategies, weaning, sore nipples, and toxicology. If an answer to your question is not immediately at hand, they'll research it and get back to you. Referrals to local counselors and La Leche group leaders are also available. The line is open 24 hours a day.

La Leche League International
P.O. Box 1209
9616 Minneapolis Avenue
Franklin Park, IL 60131–8209
312-455-7730

○ **Child-Care Products**

The staff at Johnson & Johnson's information center will provide you with answers to questions about their baby products. They will also supply general information about child care. The center answers calls weekdays between 9 A.M. and 5 P.M., EST.

Johnson & Johnson Baby Product Information
Johnson & Johnson
501 George Street
New Brunswick, NJ 08901
800-526-3967
800-942-7764 (In New Jersey)

o Child Development

The Totline hotline, staffed by persons affiliated with a private mental health center, will answer any question you have about child development and behavior. When you call, you needn't give your name—the center wants to encourage parents of children with less socially acceptable difficulties (such as bed-wetting, stealing, and temper tantrums) to seek information and advice. If, by strange chance, you stump them, they'll refer you to someone who can help. Referrals to counseling agencies and physicians are available. Despite the hotline's name, the staff is prepared to handle questions concerning any child 18 years old or younger. The line is open every weekday between 9 A.M. and 4:30 P.M., EST.

Totline
Raritan Bay Mental Health Center
570 Lee
Perth Amboy, NJ 08861
201-442-1362

o Child Law

The Children's Defense Fund will provide you with information about current legislation and how it affects children. Answers to questions on a variety of issues relating to children, including health care and health problems, can be had here. Call any weekday between the hours of 9 A.M. and 5 P.M., EST.

Children's Defense Fund
122 C Street NW
Suite 400
Washington, DC 20001
800-424-9602
202-628-8787 (In Washington, DC)

○ **Exceptional Children** See *Education: Resources for the Learning Disabled and Handicapped.*

○ Missing and Exploited Children

The National Center for Missing and Exploited Children is a national clearinghouse that provides prevention and education programs for parents, schools, and community agencies; disseminates information to communities to aid in protecting children; conducts outreach programs; provides information to legislators about effective measures that ensure the safety and protection of children; and assists individuals, groups, and state and local governments in investigating and prosecuting cases of criminally and sexually exploited children. If you have information that could lead to the location and recovery of a missing child, call the 800 number listed below. (Because these calls literally can be a matter of life or death, the center asks that the hotline be used only by those who have critical information.) If you would like information about the problem of missing and exploited children, call the 202 number listed below. The hotline is answered 24 hours a day; the clearinghouse is open 9 A.M. to 5 P.M., EST.

National Center for Missing and Exploited
  Children
1835 K Street NW
Suite 700
Washington, DC 20006
202-634-9836
Hotline: **800-843-LOST**

The following numbers will put you in touch with an international locator service for missing children. The toll-free number is for those who have spotted or located a missing child; the local number should be used by people who want to register a missing child. Both lines are answered 24 hours a day, every day of the week.

Childfind
P.O. Box 277
New Paltz, NY 12561
800-426-5678
914-255-1848 (In New York)

o Nutrition

The Nutrition Action Group, founded by writer and physician Tom Brewer, operates a 24-hour hotline for pregnant women, their families, childbirth educators, midwives, and doctors. Their primary areas of interest include nutrition, malnutrition, toxemia of pregnancy, eclampsia, high blood pressure, swelling, nausea and vomiting, drugs, premature labor, and sodium and protein levels during pregnancy. They also answer questions from lawyers involved in malpractice cases that involve these issues.

Nutrition Action Group (NAG)
2023 Oak Street
San Francisco, CA 94117
415-752-7934

The Beech-Nut Nutrition Hotline has a library of over forty tapes prepared by doctors, dentists, and nutritionists that answer questions about colic and other common child disorders. A consumer relations agent (at the same number) will personally discuss nutritional requirements, menu plans, child development, prenatal and postnatal care, and, of course, stages of use for Beech-Nut products. Upon request, Beech-Nut will send you guides to nutrition and allergy control. The hotline is in operation weekdays from 9 A.M. to 6 P.M., EST.

Beech-Nut Nutrition Hotline
Beech-Nut Corporation
P.O. Box 127
Fort Washington, PA 19034
800-523-6633
800-492-2384 (In Pennsylvania)

O Poisoning See *Poison Control Centers.*

O Runaways

Volunteers at the Runaway Hotline are a life line to distressed children and teenagers; they connect runaways with local sources of food, shelter, and health care, act as go-betweens for children and parents, and set up conference calls with appropriate social agencies. They will also contact parents of runaways at the request of the child. Call the hotline any time; the phones are answered 24 hours a day, seven days a week.

Runaway Hotline
Box 12428
Austin, TX 78711
800-231-6946

The staff at the National Runaway Switchboard provide counseling and assistance to runaways. If you need shelter, they'll direct you to a place in your area to spend the night. The hotline is answered 24 hours a day, but it is often busy, so keep trying.

National Runaway Switchboard
2210 N. Halsted
Chicago, IL 60614
800-621-4000

o Sexual Abuse

Founded in 1974, the Illusion Theater serves as a national clearinghouse for information and referrals on education, resources, and programs directed at the prevention of sexual abuse. The staff members are eager to help human-service professionals, treatment and education systems, health-care providers, legislators, and parents with technical assistance and consultation. Originally created to use theater to educate children and adults about sexual abuse prevention, the theater currently has three programs available: "Touch," an award-winning presentation geared toward elementary-age children; "No Easy Answers," a theatrical presentation developed for adolescents to help them explore sexual development and abuse prevention skills; and "For Adults Only," a prevention play designed to help adults examine some of the areas where sex and violence are confused. However, the theater staff can help implement programs without the use of educational theater. Publications of interest to educators, parents, and abused children are also available. For more information, call the theater any weekday between 8:30 A.M. and 4:30 P.M., CST.

Illusion Theater
304 Washington Avenue North
Minneapolis, MN 55401
612-339-4944

VOICES, a group founded in 1980 by women who had experienced sexual victimization by a family member as a child, has two primary goals: to help victims of incest become survivors and to generate awareness among the community of the prevalence of incest, its impact, and how it can be prevented. VOICES sees its role not so much as an advice-giving agency but rather as one that helps survivors help each other. As such, they have a vast list of self-help groups, therapists, and therapy groups around the country who specialize in helping survivors, and they sponsor special interest groups for those who have experienced exceptional variations of incest and for mothers of children who were abused. Their bibliographic file of over 600 items is available to both survivors and scholars. VOICES encourages women and men to call anytime. If you get the answering machine, leave your name and telephone number; someone will get back to you within 24 hours.

Victims of Incest Can Emerge Survivors
   (VOICES)
P.O. Box 148309
Chicago, IL 60614
312-327-1500

The sole purpose of Incest Survivors Anonymous (ISA) is to help incest survivors who want to deal positively with the repercussions of the emotional, mental, spiritual, and physical damage done when they were victimized. Founded in 1980 by an incest survivor, the program is based on the Twelve Steps and Twelve Traditions of Alcoholics Anonymous. Groups are open to women, girls, boys, and men—anyone, in other words, who wants to work toward recognizing the destructive coping mechanisms cultivated in youth and who strives to break free to a new understanding of self. Pro-survivors are also welcome. If you'd like more information on ISA or would like the telephone number of the group nearest you, call the number listed below anytime. If you get the machine, leave your name, telephone number, and a brief message, and someone will get back to you within 24 hours.

Incest Survivors Anonymous
P.O. Box 5613
Long Beach, CA 90805–0613
213-422-1632

○ Single Parents

Parents Without Partners (PWP) is a self-help group that will provide information on child support to single parents, their children, and all other interested parties. They will also refer you to PWP chapters throughout the United States and Canada. Call weekdays from 8:30 A.M. to 5 P.M., EST; or leave a message on the answering machine after hours and someone will get back to you.

Parents Without Partners (PWP)
7910 Woodmont Avenue
Bethesda, MD 20814
800-638-8078
301-654-8850 (In Maryland)

○ Sudden Infant Death Syndrome   See *Health: Sudden Infant Death Syndrome.*

• CIVIC CONCERNS   (See also *Children and Child Care: Sexual Abuse; Environmental Issues.*)

○ General Information

If you're concerned about a civic problem but need help getting started, call Civitex, an organization that collects and provides information on innovations and techniques used by other citizen groups and municipal government organizations to address local problems. Civitex also helps callers share and learn about methods of financing, advocacy, volunteer recruitment, leadership training, and organizational structure. Projects are coded in their computer by keywords such as "beautification," "food banks," "abandoned property," and "noise." Profiles of citizen-action projects in areas such as community economic development, government reform, health, and the environment are also available. Government officials, nonprofit groups, academics, journalists, and concerned citizens are encouraged to call any weekday between 9 A.M. and 5 P.M., EST.

Citizen's Forum on Self-Government
Civitex Information Service
55 W. 43d Street
New York, NY 10036
800-223-6004
212-730-7930 (In New York, Alaska, and
    Hawaii)

○ **Volunteering** See *Volunteering.*

• CIVIL RIGHTS

○ Civil Rights Hotline

If you feel you have been discriminated against in any way on the basis of your race, color, national origin, handicap, or age, call the Civil Rights Hotline. The staff will investigate your claim and suggest strategies for action. This office does not handle sex discrimination complaints or inquiries. (*See* Law: Discrimination.) The office is open every weekday from 9 A.M. to 5:30 P.M., EST.

Civil Rights Hotline
Department of Health and Human Services
Office of Civil Rights
330 Independence Avenue SW
Room 5514 North Building
Washington, DC 20201
800-368-1019
202-863-0100 (In Washington, DC)

○ **Discrimination** See *Law: Discrimination.*

○ Housing Discrimination

If you feel you've been discriminated against while shopping for a place to live, call the Department of Housing and Urban Development's (HUD's) Housing Discrimination Hotline. A staff member will offer advice, take down the details of your complaint, and provide you with information. The line is open weekdays from 8 A.M. to 8 P.M., EST. After hours, you may leave a message on the answering machine, and someone will get back to you the next working day.

Housing Discrimination Hotline
U.S. Department of Housing and Urban
   Development
Office of Fair Housing and Equal Opportunity
451 7th Street SW
Washington, DC 20410–5500
800-424-8590
202-426-3500 (In Washington, DC)

○ Lesbian and Gay Rights See *Information Centers: Lesbians and Gays; Law: Lesbians and Gays.*

○ Nonsmokers' Rights

Action on Smoking and Health (ASH) is a national, nonprofit charitable organization that serves as the legal-action arm of the antismoking community, ensuring that the voice of the nonsmoker is heard (the organization was founded by John Banzhaf, the attorney who effectively drove cigarette commercials off television and compelled the networks to make free time available for antismoking messages). The staff will provide you with information about the antismoking campaign as well as detail smoking hazards and nonsmokers' rights. Information to employers about establishing and implementing a no-smoking policy in the workplace is also available. Call any weekday between 8 A.M. and 4:30 P.M., EST.

Action on Smoking and Health (ASH)
2013 H Street NW
Washington, DC 20006
202-659-4310

○ **Women's Rights**   (See also *Information Centers: Women; Law: Women.*)

If you feel you have been barred from a job or educational opportunity because you are female, call the Office of Civil Rights within the Department of Education. A staff member will direct you to a regional office that can investigate your claim. Call weekdays between 8:30 A.M. and 5 P.M., EST.

Department of Education
Office of Civil Rights
330 C Street SW
Washington, DC 20202
202-732-1213

• COLLECTIBLES

○ Art Appraisals

For a $30 fee, Barden Prisant, the Yale-trained art expert in charge of the appraisal service Telepraisal, will give you computerized information regarding the value and marketability of a specific work of art. He can also give you information on buying and authenticating works of art. The fee is payable by credit card or check, and the information will be read to you over the telephone or printed out and sent by mail, as you prefer. The telephone is answered weekdays between 9 A.M. and 5 P.M., EST.

Telepraisal
500 Old Country Road
Garden City, NY 11530
800-645-6002
516-747-8730 (In New York)

o Baseball Cards

Peter Dehart, a collector and scholar, began collecting base-ball cards nearly twenty years ago from a sense of nostalgia and from a desire to hold on to some of the values and feel-ings—including accomplishment, pride, effort, and inno-cence—that were once an important part of the game. When you call, he will provide you with anecdotal information about the players and their cards (he collects mainly those from the 1950s), point up the artistic merit of various cards, and detail the value of both contemporary and antique cards. De-hart believes that the changes in the cards over the years reflect changes in society (cards printed after World War II, he says, were written in militaristic and patriotic language; today's cards are sterile and cold, perhaps reflecting the con-temporary ambience of the game). Dehart will share his phi-losophy and answer your questions on cards and collecting any weekday from 8 A.M. to 5 P.M., EST.

Peter J. Dehart
Instructional Services Dispatcher-Scheduler
Pennsylvania State University
Capitol Campus
Route 230
Middletown, PA 17057
717-948-6224

o Coins and Currency

This office of the Treasury Department designs, engraves, and prints currency, bonds, notes, bills, certificates, stamps, and security documents and will provide you with answers to any questions you have about the history, design, or engraving of currency. Call any weekday between 8:30 A.M. and 4:30 P.M., EST.

Bureau of Engraving and Printing
Treasury Department
14th and C Streets
Washington, DC 20228
202-447-0193

o Jewelry Appraisals

Want to know whether the ring your grandmother left you twenty years ago has appreciated in value? Call the American Gem Society, an organization founded in 1934 for the advancement of the jewelry industry and for the protection of the consumer. The society will provide you with straight information on appraisals as well as answer your questions about jewelry making, jewelry care, and gold and gem investing. These qualified gemologists will also provide you with the name and address of the nearest accredited gem laboratory and member jeweler. Call weekdays between 8:30 A.M. and 5 P.M., PST.

American Gem Society
5901 W. 3d Street
Los Angeles, CA 90036
213-936-4367

o Stamps

If you need information on the subject, design, history, or availability of various stamps, call the U.S. Postal Service Stamps Division. They'll provide you with all the information they have and give you a few pointers on collecting stamps. The staff asks that callers restrict their inquiries to philatelic concerns; complaints are handled by the Office of Consumer Affairs (see *Postal Service: Complaints*). The office is open every weekday from 8 A.M. to 5 P.M., EST.

U.S. Postal Service
Stamps Division
475 L'Enfant Plaza SW
Washington, DC 20260
202-245-4951

• COMPUTERS

○ Diskettes

If you're having trouble figuring out which end of your 3M diskette is up, call one of the service agents at the number listed below. Not only will they answer your questions about the proper use of diskettes, they will also explain your diskette's compatibility, or incompatibility, with other systems. Call on weekdays from 8:30 A.M. to 4:30 P.M., CST.

3M Data Recording Products Division
St. Paul, MN 55144
800-328-9438
612-736-9524 (In Minnesota)

○ Software

"Computer access through a human interface"—that's a quote. Translated, it means that when you call the Software Inquiry Service (SIS) a computer consultant will scan a data base for software that meets your specifications and offer you a free, brief review. Summaries of more than 28,000 software packages (many based on SIS's own evaluations) are available as well as information on SIS information services. The line operates weekdays from 9 A.M. to 6 P.M., CST.

Software Inquiry Service (SIS)
4730 Dakota Street
Prior Lake, MN 55372
800-328-0196
612-447-6959 (In Minnesota)

○ Special Education Systems

The Special Education Software Center is a national center with an electronic network system that serves as a clearing-house for anyone interested in computers and special education. The staff counsels teachers, parents, and administrators on selecting and using appropriate software for special education students and suggests ways to modify software to make it more suitable to these students. The center can also help you stay up-to-date on the major issues covered at the annual Special Education Software Conference. The lines are open 24 hours a day.

The center is now accessible on-line for those who wish to dial up the center with their own modem and telecommunications software; 800-435-7639 provides free access to the center (except for residents of Alaska and Hawaii).

Special Education Software Center
SRI International
Building B, Room S312
333 Ravenswood Avenue
Menlo Park, CA 94025

For technical assistance:
800-223-2711

For software information:
800-327-5892

• CONSUMER COMPLAINT SERVICES

○ General Complaints and Inquiries

The U.S. Department of Commerce's Consumer Affairs division handles consumer questions and complaints about business. The staff advises businesses on how to be responsive to consumer needs and improve customer relations by using easy-to-understand language on product labels; the staff also provides information to consumers and businesses about government policies and programs that affect commerce in the United States. Call any weekday between 8:30 A.M. and 5 P.M., EST.

U.S. Department of Commerce
Consumer Affairs
Main Commerce Building
Washington, DC 20230
202-377-5001

The Better Business Bureaus, dedicated to building public trust in the business system, are fact-finding organizations that investigate and act on complaints of unfair and unethical business practices. If you want to register a complaint about a local business, check your local telephone directory for the BBB office nearest you. If you are unable to locate one in your area, dial the number listed below; a staff member will help you any weekday between 9 A.M. and 5 P.M., EST.

Council of Better Business Bureaus
1515 Wilson Boulevard
Arlington, VA 22209
703-276-0100

It all started when B. L. Ochman was studying for her first-year exams at the University of Bridgeport. She bought a bag of Tootsie Roll pops, and when she got home she discovered that there weren't any tootsies in the pops. Never one to grow queasy over making a fuss, she wrote a letter. As a result, she received a carton stuffed with Tootsie Roll pops in the mail. Ochman has turned her kvetching panache into a business (would it be wrong to call it a social service agency?). For a modest fee, Ochman will complain to anybody about almost anything, be it an appliance company that refuses to replace your faulty microwave or a roommate who will not keep his dirty socks off your pillow. "Just because you buy a lemon," she says, "you shouldn't get squeezed." Ochman will be happy to consider your complaint any weekday between 9 A.M. and 5 P.M., EST.

Rent-a-Kvetch
10 E. 21st Street
Suite 1110
New York, NY 10010
212-982-0684

O Direct-Mail Marketing

If you're being harassed by a direct-mail marketing company
or would like to register a complaint against one, call this
hotline. They will record the details of your complaint and
try to obtain satisfaction from the company involved. The
staff can also help remove your name from an unwanted mailing list and will offer suggestions for handling unsolicited telephone sales calls. Call any weekday from 9 A.M. to noon and
from 2 P.M. to 5 P.M., EST.

The Mail Order Action Line
6 E. 43d Street
New York, NY 10017
212-689-4977

O Funeral Complaints and Inquiries See *Death and Dying: Funeral Complaints and Inquiries.*

O Magazine Subscription Complaints

Whether or not your subscription was ordered through Publishers' Clearinghouse, its staff will help you with any kind
of complaint you have about your magazine subscription, be
it incorrect billing or late arrivals. The hotline is open weekdays from 9 A.M. to 5 P.M., EST.

Magazine Action Hotline
Publishers' Clearinghouse
382 Channel Drive
Port Washington, NY 11050
800-645-9242
516-883-5432 (In New York state)

O New York City See *New York City: Consumer Services.*

○ **Postal Service** See *Postal Service: Complaints.*

○ **Product Information** See *Information Centers: Product Information.*

○ **Travel Complaints** See *Travel: Air Passenger Complaints; Travel: Bus and Rail Passenger Complaints; Travel: Complaints against Travel Suppliers.*

● **COOKING** See *Diet and Nutrition.*

● **CRAFTS** (See also *Collectibles; Gardens and Gardening.*)

○ **General Information**

The expert staff at the American Crafts Council (ACC) Library will provide you with answers to your questions about the history of crafts both in the United States and in other nations. How-to information about popular arts, including macramé, body painting, and hair ornamentation, may also be obtained here. Call Tuesday through Friday between 10 A.M. and 5 P.M., EST.

American Crafts Council Library
44 W. 53d Street
New York, NY 10019
212-869-9462

○ **Woodworking** See *Home Maintenance: Woodworking.*

D

• DEATH AND DYING

○ Children   See *Children and Child Care: Bereaved Parents and Siblings.*

○ Funeral Arrangements

This federation of nonprofit, nonsectarian consumer organizations provides information to the general public and works to protect every person's right to freedom of choice in making funeral arrangements. When you call, a staff member will help you evaluate undertakers' services and prepayment plans and offer you guidance about joining a memorial society that provides low-cost funerals. Information about alternatives to traditional funerals may also be obtained here. Call any weekday between 9:30 A.M. and 5:30 P.M., EST.

Continental Association of Funeral and
  Memorial Societies
2001 S Street NW
Suite 530
Washington, DC 20009
202-745-0634

○ Funeral Complaints and Inquiries

If you think the undertaker has rooked you, call ThanaCAP. Not only can the staff provide you with facts and figures, but it will also help mediate if a dispute develops. Although ThanaCAP is funded by the National Funeral Directors Association, its members are all consumer advocates unaffiliated with the industry. The phone is answered weekdays from 8 A.M. to 4:30 P.M., CST.

ThanaCAP
11121 W. Oklahoma Avenue
Milwaukee, WI 53227
414-541-7925

o Hospices

The staff at the National Hospice Organization will provide individuals, families, researchers, and members of the news media with information on hospices and hospice programs around the country. Referrals to hospices within your area are also available. Call any weekday between 9 A.M. and 6 P.M., EST.

National Hospice Organization
1901 N. Fort Myer Drive
Suite 902
Arlington, VA 22209
703-243-5900

o Living Wills

Concern for Dying is an educational council whose two primary goals are to ensure patient autonomy in regard to treatment during terminal illness and to prevent needless suffering and the futile prolongation of life through advanced medical technology. When you call, a staff member will provide you with information about living wills (legally effective declarations prohibiting extraordinary measures to prolong life), legislation affecting living wills, insurance coverage, and student programs. Publications, films, and speakers are also available. Call any weekday between 9 A.M. and 5 P.M., EST.

Concern for Dying
250 W. 57th Street, Room 831
New York, NY 10107
212-246-6962

• DIET AND NUTRITION

○ General Information

The Nutrition Information Center, designed to serve as a resource in clinical nutrition, nutrition research, and general nutrition, will answer specific questions about nutrition, provide educational materials, make referrals, and assist in program planning. Patient information sheets focusing on controversial and new areas of interest in nutrition are also available. If by chance they can't answer your question, they'll refer you to someone who can. Telephone requests are received weekdays between 9 A.M. and 5 P.M., EST.

The Nutrition Information Center
The New York Hospital-Cornell Medical
 Center
Memorial Sloan-Kettering Cancer Center
515 E. 71st Street
Room 904
New York, NY 10021
212-472-6958

"Nutrition and Diet Tips" is a prerecorded message, sponsored by the New York City Health Department's Bureau of Nutrition; it offers detailed nutritional guidelines about vitamins, fiber, balanced meals, and recipes. When you call, have a pencil and paper by your side: the nutritionist speaks quickly, and the machine does not respond to demands for patience. Nonetheless, the *schav* I made from the bureau's recipe was delicious, and when I called a week later, I got some helpful information about vitamin A. The machine is prepared to answer calls 24 hours a day, and the message is changed every Tuesday and Friday.

"Nutrition and Diet Tips"
New York City Health Department's
 Bureau of Nutrition
93 Worth Street
New York, NY 10013
212-431-4540

○ **Anorexia and Bulimia** See *Health: Anorexia and Bulimia.*

○ **Child Nutrition** See *Children and Child Care: Nutrition.*

○ Cooking the Holiday Bird

This hotline, operated by staffers who have undergone grueling training in buying, basting, stuffing, carving, and storing, will answer any question you have about preparing the holiday bird. The line is open 24 hours a day, from the beginning of November through the end of December. Although the hotline seems to have a built-in bias toward Swift Butterball turkeys, the operators will also answer questions about geese, chicken, and Cornish hens.

The Butterball Turkey Talk-Line
Swift and Company, Inc.
115 W. Jackson Boulevard
Chicago, IL 60604–3505
800-323-4848

○ Cooking Utensils

The staff at the Cookware Manufacturers Association will provide you with information on the qualities, properties, and uses of both metal and nonmetal cooking utensils. The staff can also supply you with information about caring for each type of utensil. Publications are available on request. Call any weekday between 8 A.M. and 4:30 P.M., CST.

Cookware Manufacturers Association
P.O. Box J
Walworth, WI 53184
414-275-6838

○ Dairy Products

If you've got a question about milk, butter, cheese, yogurt, or ice cream, call the National Dairy Council. The staff will try to answer any question you have about milk and dairy products weekdays between 8:30 A.M. and 4:30 P.M., CST (closed for yogurt break between noon and 1 P.M.). If time permits, staff members will also answer questions about nutrition in general.

National Dairy Council
6300 N. River Road
Rosemont, IL 60018
312-696-1020

O Food Additives

The Federation of Homemakers is a voluntary organization of concerned individuals who came together out of a mutual need to inform homemakers of potential damage wrought by chemically treated foods and consumer items such as cheese, orange juice, peanut butter, baby food, and fluoridated water. Currently, their primary area of interest is the effects of caffeine on children. The staff can also provide you with general information about recently passed laws that affect foods, drugs, and cosmetics. Call weekdays between 11 A.M. and 5 P.M., EST.

Federation of Homemakers
P.O. Box 5571
Arlington, VA 22205
703-524-4866

O Fruits and Vegetables

The United Fresh Fruit and Vegetable Association is an organization of growers, shippers, wholesalers, retailers, importers, and exporters involved in the production and marketing of fresh fruits and vegetables. Its staff will provide you with information on the nutritional value of fruits and vegetables. Seasonal buying information is also available as are tips on the care and preservation of fruits and vegetables. Inquiries are accepted every weekday between 9 A.M. and 5 P.M., EST.

United Fresh Fruit and Vegetable Association
727 N. Washington Street
Alexandria, VA 22314
202-836-3410

○ **Heart Disease Diets** See *Health: Heart Disease.*

○ **Low-Calorie Recipes**

"Dial-A-Diet-Recipe" is a prerecorded message that offers a different low-calorie recipe (the day I phoned, it was barbecue sauce) for anything from soup to nuts every day. The instructions are easy to understand, and the message is easy to hear. A behavior-modification hint or exercise tip is offered along with each recipe. The line is open 24 hours a day, every day of the year.

"Dial-A-Diet-Recipe"
Lean Line, Inc.
151 New World Way
South Plainfield, NJ 07080
201-668-0333

○ **Meat and Poultry**

You suspect that the steak marked $9.98 a pound at your supermarket is actually a much cheaper cut of meat than the label claims. Or it has a strange chemical odor. Or, upon unwrapping it, you discover that it appears stale. The trained staff at the Meat and Poultry Hotline (maintained by the U.S. Department of Agriculture) can probably help. They will answer any questions you have about labeling, wholesomeness, and storage. Experts are on hand to deal with your inquiries or complaints weekdays from 8 A.M. to 4:30 P.M., EST.

Meat and Poultry Hotline
U.S. Department of Agriculture
Room 1165, South Building
Washington, DC 20250
800-535-4555
202-472-4485 (In Washington, DC)

O Peanuts

The National Peanut Council is an organization of peanut growers, shellers, brokers, and "manufacturers" that will provide callers with information on the economic and nutritional value of peanuts. Details of the vitamins and minerals found in peanuts as well as growing information, consumption statistics, and production statistics can also be had here. Members of both the professional and lay communities are welcome to call any weekday between 9 A.M. and 5 P.M., EST.

National Peanut Council
101 S. Peyton Street
Alexandria, VA 22314
703-838-9500

O Shellfish

The staff at Crawford Lobster Company is eager to answer queries regarding New England shellfish and their seasonal variations and to suggest best buys. Company-made fish chowders, canned fish, and fish-related sporting items are also available through this number. Call any day between 8 A.M. and 5:30 P.M., EST.

Lobster Watch
62 Badgers Island
Kittery, ME 03904
800-343-4000
207-439-0930 (In Maine)

O Spirits (See also *Health: Alcoholism.*)

Dying for flambéed bananas but afraid of burning the house down? Call the Distilled Spirits Council of the United States. The council will provide you with information on safe and moderate use of alcohol in cooking as well as general information on many alcohol-related issues. Statistics based on consumption are also available as is information on responsible drinking. The council stresses that it is neither a referral nor a counseling agency and asks that callers respect the bounds of the council's interests. For more information, call any weekday between 9 A.M. and 5 P.M., EST.

Distilled Spirits Council of
the United States
1250 Eye Street NW
Washington, DC 20005
202-628-3544

o Sugar

The recipe calls for white sugar, and you've only got brown. Can you switch? Call the Sugar Association and find out. The staff of the association, whose members include sugar processors, growers, refiners, and planters, will offer information on sugar consumption, calories, sugar use in cooking, and sugar in prepackaged foods. Believe it or not, the staff will also give you information on health problems such as diabetes, obesity, and tooth decay, where, as they say, sugar "may" be implicated. The line is open every weekday from 9 A.M. to 5 P.M., EST.

Sugar Association
1511 K Street NW
Washington, DC 20005
202-628-0189

o Vegetarianism

Although the staff of the North American Vegetarian Society will pass on basic information about vegetarianism, the society views itself primarily as a referral service that provides consumers with information about locating vegetarian restaurants, groups, books, and events. A vegetarian will be happy to help you any weekday between 9 A.M. and 5 P.M., EST.

North American Vegetarian Society
P.O. Box 72
Dolgeville, NY 13329
518-568-7970

• DOMESTIC VIOLENCE HOTLINES

More and more women are realizing that there *are* alternatives to staying in a violent domestic situation. If you are attacked, most crisis counselors recommend that you try to remember five things:

1. No matter what your attacker says or does, remember that you are a valuable person who deserves protection.
2. Protect yourself, especially your stomach and head.
3. Call for help. Scream. If you can, run to the nearest person or home.
4. Get away. The personal safety of you and your children is paramount; custody and property matters can be dealt with later.
5. Call the local crisis hotline (listed by state below) to find out about a shelter in your area. A staff member will provide you with emergency food, housing, and clothing; economic assistance; job training; help with the legal and medical systems; transportation; child care; and time to think about separation, divorce, child support and custody, and housing.

Alabama Coalition against
Domestic Violence
(24 hours) **205-767-3076**
(Collect)

Alaska Network on Domestic
Violence and Sexual
Assault
(8 A.M. to 8 P.M., weekdays)
907-586-3650

Arizona Coalition against
Domestic Violence
(24 hours) **602-258-5344**

Arkansas Coalition against
Violence to Women and
Children
(24 hours) **501-442-9811**
(Collect)

Southern California
Coalition on Battered
Women
(9 A.M. to 5 P.M., weekdays)
213-392-9874 (Collect)

Northern California Shelter
Support Services
(24 hours) **415-342-0850**
(Collect)

Central California Coalition on Domestic Violence
(8 A.M. to 5 P.M., weekdays)
209-575-7037

Colorado Domestic Violence Coalition
(24 hours) **303-394-2810**

Connecticut Task Force on Abused Women
(24 hours) **203-524-5890** (Collect)

Delaware Battered Women's Hotline
(24 hours—New Castle County)
302-762-6110

Delaware Families in Transition
(24 hours—Kent and Sussex Counties)
302-422-8058 or **302-856-4919** (Collect)

District of Columbia
My Sister's Place
(24 hours) **202-529-5991**

Florida Women in Distress
(24 hours) **305-467-6333** or **800-342-9152**

Georgia Network against Domestic Violence
(24 hours) **404-536-5860** (Collect)

Hawaii: No statewide coalition; check local phone directory under "Sexual Assault," "Rape," or "Women." If you cannot find any listing, call the local police.

Idaho Council on Domestic Violence
(8:30 A.M. to 3:30 P.M., weekdays except Friday
208-334-2480

Illinois Coalition against Domestic Violence
(8:30 A.M. to 5 P.M., weekdays) **217-789-2830**

Indiana Coalition against Domestic Violence
(8 A.M. to 5 P.M., weekdays)
812-334-8378 (Collect)

Iowa Coalition against Domestic Violence
(8 A.M. to 4:30 P.M., weekdays) **515-243-6147**

Kansas Association of Domestic Violence Programs
(24 hours) **800-257-2255**

Kentucky Domestic Violence Association/ Women's Crisis Center
(24 hours) **606-491-3335** (Collect)

Louisiana Coalition against Domestic Violence/ Associated Catholic Charities
(8:30 A.M. to 5 P.M., weekdays) **504-523-3755**

Maine Family Violence Assistance Project
(24 hours) **207-623-3569** (Collect)

Maryland Network against Domestic Violence
(24 hours) **301-224-1321**

Massachusetts Coalition of Battered Women's Service Groups
(9 A.M. to 5 P.M., weekdays) **617-426-8492** (Collect)

Michigan Coalition against Domestic Violence: Harbor Hotline
(24 hours) **800-292-3925**

Minnesota Women of Nations
(24 hours) **612-646-0994**

Mississippi Coalition against Domestic Violence
(24 hours) **601-435-1968** (Collect)

Missouri Women's Self-Help Center
(24 hours—eastern U.S.) **314-531-2003**

Missouri Rose Brooks Center
(24 hours—western U.S.) **816-861-6100**

Montana Coalition against Domestic Violence/Great Falls Crisis Center
(24 hours) **406-453-6511**

Nebraska Task Force on Domestic Violence and Sexual Assault
(9 A.M. to 5 P.M., weekdays) **402-471-3121**

Nevada Network against Domestic Violence
(9 A.M. to 5 P.M., weekdays) **702-358-4214**

New Hampshire Coalition against Domestic and Sexual Violence
(24 hours) **800-852-3311**
(9 A.M. to 5 P.M., weekdays, but gives more information) **603-224-8893** (Collect)

New Jersey Women's Referral Central
(24 hours) **800-322-8092**

New Mexico Coalition against Domestic Violence/La Casa
(24 hours) **505-526-6661** (Collect)

New York State Domestic
Violence Hotline
(24 hours) **800-942-6906**
New York State Bilingual
Domestic Violence Hot-
line—in Spanish
(9 A.M. to 5 P.M., weekdays)
800-942-6908

North Carolina Coalition of
Domestic Violence
Programs
(8 A.M. to 10 P.M., weekdays,
with machine giving
information after hours)
704-786-9317

North Dakota Council on
Abused Women's Services:
Domestic Violence
Hotline
(24 hours) **800-472-2911**

Ohio Womanshelter
(24 hours) **216-297-9999**
(Collect)

Oklahoma Domestic
Violence Safeline
(24 hours) **800-522-7233**

Oregon Coalition against
Domestic and Sexual
Violence/Portland
Women's Crisis Line
(24 hours) **503-235-5333**
(Collect)

Pennsylvania Coalition
against Domestic Violence
(9 A.M. to 5 P.M., weekdays)
800-932-4632

Puerto Rico: No statewide
coalition; check local
phone directory under
"Sexual Assault," "Rape,"
or "Women." If you
cannot find any listing, call
the local police.

Rhode Island Council on
Domestic Violence
(24 hours) **401-723-3051**
(Collect)

South Carolina Coalition
against Domestic Violence
and Sexual Assault/
Sistercare Crisis and
Information Line
(24 hours) **803-765-9428**
(Collect)

South Dakota Coalition
against Domestic Violence
(24 hours) **605-226-1212**
(Collect)

Tennessee Coalition against
Domestic Violence: Safe
Space Hotline
(24 hours) **615-623-3125**
(Collect)

Texas Council on Family
Violence
(9 A.M. to 5 P.M., weekdays)
512-482-8200 (Collect)

Utah Domestic Violence
Crisis Hotline
(24 hours) **801-355-2804**

Vermont Domestic Violence
Program
(24 hours) **802-775-3232**

Virginians against Domestic
Violence
(24 hours) **804-643-0888**

Washington Domestic
Violence Hotline
(24 hours) **800-562-6025**

West Virginia Coalition
against Domestic Violence
(24 hours) **304-645-6334**
(Collect)

Wisconsin Coalition against
Woman Abuse
(9 A.M. to 4 P.M., weekdays)
608-255-0539 (Collect)

Milwaukee Task Force on
Battered Women
(24 hours) **414-643-5455**
(Collect)
Will refer women to local
"safe spaces" throughout
the state.

Wyoming Family Violence
and Sexual Assault
Statewide Referral
(24 hours) **800-442-8337**

E

• EDUCATION

○ Advanced-Placement Tests

College Board is, without a doubt, the best place to turn for information about advanced-placement (AP) courses and AP exams. The staff will also give you information about sources of financial assistance and will help you estimate your college costs. Call weekdays between 9 A.M. and 5 P.M., EST.

College Board
888 Seventh Avenue
New York, NY 10106
212-582-6210

○ Art, Theater, Dance, and Music Programs

If you're wondering whether the art, theater, dance, or music program you're interested in is officially accredited, call the National Association number listed below. Besides accrediting information, some general information about education programs and opportunities is also available. The office is open weekdays from 9 A.M. to 5 P.M., EST.

National Association of Schools of Art and
   Design, Theatre, Dance, and Music
11250 Roger Bacon Drive
Reston, VA 22090
202-437-0700

○ Computers for the Handicapped See *Computers: Special Education Systems.*

○ Correspondence Schools

If you're wondering whether the correspondence school you're interested in is legitimate, call the National Home Study Council. In all likelihood, if the school is reliable, it's been accredited by the council. Their entire list of seventy-seven non-degree-granting correspondence schools throughout the United States is free and will be mailed on request. Call weekdays 9 A.M. to 5 P.M., EST.

National Home Study Council
1601 18th Street NW
Washington, DC 20009
202-234-5100

If you're looking for information about how to get a master's or bachelor's degree at home, call the National University Continuing Education Association. The association will provide you with information on every home-study course offered by accredited colleges and universities in the United States. Their updated list is available on request for about $6. The staff is available on weekdays from 9 A.M. to 5 P.M., EST.

National University Continuing Education
    Association
1 Dupont Circle
Suite 420
Washington, DC 20036
202-659-3130

○ Educational Resources

ERIC, the educational information system sponsored by the National Institute of Education within the U.S. Department of Education, is designed to provide users with ready access to (primarily) English-language literature dealing with various aspects of education. If you have a general question about any aspect of education, call Central ERIC (listed below). More substantive inquiries should be directed to the particular clearinghouse covering your area of interest. A charge is usually levied for computer searches; otherwise the information is free. Referrals to other organizations are also available.

Educational Resources Information Center
  (ERIC) (also known as Central ERIC)
1200 19th Street NW
Washington, DC 20208
(8 A.M. to 5:30 P.M., EST, weekdays)
  202-254-5500

ERIC Clearinghouse on Adult, Career, and
  Vocational Education (CE)
Ohio State University
National Center for Research in Vocational
  Education
1960 Kenny Road
Columbus, OH 43210
(8 A.M. to 5 P.M., EST, weekdays) **614-486-3655**
Summer hours:
7:30 A.M. to 4:30 P.M., EST, weekdays
Information about all levels and settings of adult and continuing, career, and vocational and technical education. Adult education ranges from basic literacy training to professional skill upgrading. Career education includes career awareness, career decision making, and career change. Vocational and technical education includes new subprofessional fields, industrial arts, corrections education, employment and training programs, entrepreneurship, and adult retraining.

ERIC Clearinghouse on Counseling and
  Personnel Services (CG)
University of Michigan
School of Education, Room 2108
Ann Arbor, MI 48109
(8 A.M. to 5 P.M., EST, weekdays) **313-764-9492**
Summer hours:
7:30 A.M. to 4 P.M., EST, weekdays
Information about preparation, practice, and supervision of counselors at all educational levels and in all settings and theoretical development of counseling and guidance; personnel procedures, group work, and case work; personnel work-

ers and their relation to career planning, family consultations, and student-orientation activities.

ERIC Clearinghouse on Educational
  Management (EA)
University of Oregon
1787 Agate Street
Eugene, OR 97403
(8 A.M. to 5 P.M., PST, weekdays) **503-686-5043**
Information on the leadership, management, and structure of public and private educational organizations; practice and theory of administration; preservice and in-service preparation of administrators; methods of organization. This includes sites, buildings, and equipment for education and planning, financing, constructing, renovating, maintaining, and insuring educational facilities.

ERIC Clearinghouse on Elementary and Early
  Childhood Education (PS)
University of Illinois
College of Education
805 W. Pennsylvania Avenue
Urbana, IL 61801
(8 A.M. to noon and 1 P.M. to 5 P.M., CST,
  weekdays) **217-333-1386**
Information on the physical, cognitive, social, educational, and cultural development of children from birth through early adolescence; prenatal factors; parental behavior factors; learning-theory research and practice related to the development of young children; and theoretical and philosophical issues pertaining to children's development and education.

ERIC Clearinghouse on Handicapped and
  Gifted Children (EC)
Council for Exceptional Children
1920 Association Drive
Reston, VA 22091
(8 A.M. to 5 P.M., EST, weekdays) **703-620-3660**
Summer hours:
8 A.M. to 5 P.M., EST, weekdays (except Friday)

Information on all aspects of the education and development of the handicapped and gifted, including prevention, identification and assessment, intervention, and enrichment, both in special settings and within the mainstream.

ERIC Clearinghouse on Higher Education (HE)
George Washington University
1 Dupont Circle NW
Suite 630
Washington, DC 20036
(9 A.M. to 5 P.M., EST, weekdays) **202-296-2597**
Information on college and university conditions, problems, programs, and students; curricular and instructional programs and institutional research at the college level; federal programs; professional education; graduate education; collegiate computer-assisted learning and management; university extension programs; management of institutions of higher education.

ERIC Clearinghouse on Information Resources
   (IR)
Syracuse University
Huntington Hall, Room 030
Syracuse, NY 13210
(8:30 A.M. to 4:30 P.M., EST, weekdays)
   315-423-3640
Educational technology and library and information science at all levels; instructional design, development, and evaluation within educational technology; computers and microcomputers; telecommunications; audiovisual materials; management of information services for education-related organizations.

ERIC Clearinghouse for Junior Colleges (JC)
University of California at Los Angeles
Mathematical Sciences Building, Room 8118
405 Hilgard Avenue
Los Angeles, CA 90024
(8 A.M. to 5 P.M., PST, weekdays) **213-825-3931**
Development, administration, and evaluation of two-year public and private community and junior colleges, technical

institutes, and two-year branch university campuses; two-year-college students, faculty, staff, curricula, programs, support services; linkages between two-year colleges and business and industrial organizations.

ERIC Clearinghouse on Languages and
  Linguistics (FL)
Center for Applied Linguistics
1118 22d Street NW
Washington, DC 20037
(9 A.M. to 5 P.M., EST, weekdays) **202-429-9292**
Summer hours:
8:30 A.M. to 5:15 P.M., EST, Monday–Thursday
  and 8:30 A.M. to 12:30 P.M., EST, Friday
Information on languages and language sciences; theoretical and applied linguistics; linguistics instruction and methodology; psycholinguistics and the psychology of language learning; cultural and intercultural context of languages; bilingualism and bilingual education; sociolinguistics; study abroad and international exchanges; teacher training; commonly and uncommonly taught languages; related curriculum developments and problems.

ERIC Clearinghouse on Reading and
  Communication Skills (CS)
National Council of Teachers of English
1111 Kenyon Road
Urbana, IL 61801
(8 A.M. to 4:30 P.M., CST, weekdays)
  217-328-3870
Information on reading, English, and communication skills, preschool through college; educational research and instruction development in reading, writing, speaking, and listening; identification, diagnosis, and remediation of reading problems; speech communication; interpersonal and small group interaction; all aspects of reading behavior with emphasis on physiology, psychology, sociology, and teaching; instructional materials, curricula, tests, and methodology; preparation of reading teachers and specialists.

ERIC Clearinghouse on Rural Education and
  Small Schools (RC)
New Mexico State University
Box 3AP
Las Cruces, NM 88003
(8 A.M. to noon and 1 P.M. to 5 P.M., MST,
  weekdays) **505-646-2623**
Information on economic, cultural, social, or other factors related to educational programs and practices for rural residents; American Indians, Alaska natives, Mexican Americans, and migrants; educational practices and programs in all small schools; outdoor education.

ERIC Clearinghouse for Science, Mathematics,
  and Environmental Education (SE)
Ohio State University
1200 Chambers Road, Room 310
Columbus, OH 43212
(8 A.M. to 5 P.M., EST, weekdays) **614-422-6717**
Summer hours:
8 A.M. to 4:30 P.M., EST, weekdays
Information about science, mathematics, and environmental education at all levels; development of curriculum and instructional materials; teachers and teacher education; learning theory and theory outcomes; research and evaluative studies; computer applications.

ERIC Clearinghouse for Social Studies/Social
  Science Education (SO)
Social Science Education Consortium, Inc.
855 Broadway
Boulder, CO 80302
(8 A.M. to 5 P.M., MST, weekdays) **303-492-8434**
Information on the content of social science disciplines; applications of theory and research to social science education; education as a social science; comparative education; content and curriculum materials on "social" topics such as law-related education, ethnic studies, bias and discrimination, aging, adoption, women's equity, and sex education.

ERIC Clearinghouse on Teacher Education
(SP)
American Association of Colleges for Teacher
Education
1 Dupont Circle NW
Suite 610
Washington, DC 20036
(8 A.M. to 5 P.M., EST, weekdays) **202-293-2450**
Information on school personnel at all levels; teacher selection
and training; preservice and in-service preparation and retirement; the theory, philosophy, and practice of teaching; curricula and general education not specifically covered by other
clearinghouses; all aspects of physical education, health education, and recreation education.

ERIC Clearinghouse on Tests, Measurements,
and Evaluation (TM)
Educational Testing Service
Rosedale Road
Princeton, NJ 08541
(8:30 A.M. to 4:45 P.M., EST, weekdays)
609-734-5176
Information on tests and other measurement devices; methodology of measurement and evaluation; application of tests,
measurement, or evaluation in educational projects or programs; research design and methodology in the area of testing
and measurement evaluation; learning theory in general.

ERIC Clearinghouse on Urban Education (UD)
Teachers College, Columbia University
Institute for Urban and Minority Education
Box 40
525 W. 120th Street
New York, NY 10027
(9 A.M. to 5 P.M., EST, weekdays) **212-678-3433**
Information about programs and practices in public, paro-
chial, and private schools in urban areas; education of particular racial- and ethnic-minority children and youth in various
settings; theory and practice of educational equity; urban and

minority experiences; urban and minority social institutions and services.

○ Films

The Educational Film Library Association is one of the friendliest and most reliable sources of information around. Not only will staff members provide information to educators about where to obtain a particular film, they'll also try to answer any question you might have about documentary and educational films, business films, animation, film as art, and independent films. The library contains over 1300 books on film, television, and audiovisual, and has special files on film festivals, library administration, grants, filmmakers, and film centers in the United States. Information about film schools and film vocabulary will also be provided. Call weekdays, from 2 P.M. to 6 P.M., EST.

Educational Film Library Association
45 John Street
New York, NY 10038
212-227-5599

○ Financial Aid

Despite the current administration's insouciance, the U.S. Department of Education is still a solid source of information about financial assistance. They're especially helpful if you've got questions about government-sponsored programs. Call any weekday from 9 A.M. to 5 P.M., EST.

U.S. Department of Education
Student Information Center
P.O. Box 84
Washington, DC 20044
301-984-4070

Anyone who's been boggled by a family financial statement should make use of the American College Testing (ACT) Student Need Analysis Service. Staff members not only will give you an idea of how much aid you can expect, they'll also give you advice on filling out those confounding papers. They can also provide you with general information about various sources of financial assistance and tell you how to apply. The line is open weekdays from 8:30 A.M. to 4:30 P.M., CST.

American College Testing Program
P.O. Box 168
Iowa City, IA 52243
319-337-1040

O Nonsexist Educational Materials   See *Information Centers: Women.*

O Programs for Older People   See *Older People: Education.*

O Programs in Sports Medicine   See *Sports and Athletics: Sports Medicine.*

O Resources for the Learning Disabled and Handicapped

Closer Look is a unique information center dedicated to strengthening opportunities for children and youth with learning disabilities to become productive adults, participating as completely as possible in the mainstream of society. Their projects include an LD Teenline, a service which responds to the educational, vocational, and psychological needs of learning-disabled adolescents, their families, and professionals who work with them; Campus Access for the Learning Disabled, a resource for information on appropriate colleges, new technology, and support services; Project Bridge, a curriculum designed to strengthen communication between parents and teachers of handicapped children; Life Skills Training Program, a curriculum designed to develop independent living skills; and Project BUILD, an information service for learning-disabled juvenile offenders in the Washington, DC, area. Information on vocational training and postsecondary opportunities is also available. Closer Look is open every weekday from 9 A.M. to 5 P.M., EST.

Closer Look®/Parents' Campaign for
  Handicapped Children and Youth
1201 16th Street NW
Washington, DC 20036
202-822-7900

The Association for Children and Adults with Learning Disabilities (ACLD) is a volunteer group of over 60,000 parents
that serves as a general resource center for information on
learning disabilities and testing programs. The staff member
I spoke with said that the staff can answer every question
from, "I think my child has a learning disability; what should
I do?" to "How can I find out what college will accept my
child?" (ACLD has a list of colleges that accept learning-disabled students.) Referrals to local sources of information and
support are also available. The office is open every weekday
from 9 A.M. to 5 P.M., EST.

Association for Children and Adults with
  Learning Disabilities (ACLD)
4156 Library Road
Pittsburgh, PA 15234
412-341-1515

The Orton Dyslexia Society is a vast information bank on
dyslexia that provides information to the public, concerned
parents, and other family members about this specific learning
disability. Guidelines for evaluating testing programs and information on tutoring programs are also available. Call any
weekday between 9 A.M. and 5 P.M., EST.

Orton Dyslexia Society
724 York Road
Baltimore, MD 21204
800-ABCD123

If your child is handicapped and you'd like information on
securing her or his right to an education, call the National
Information Center. Not only will the center provide the

names and addresses of services and resources available in your area, but it can also direct you to local support groups. The line is open every weekday from 8:30 A.M. to 5:30 P.M., EST.

National Information Center for Handicapped
  Children and Youth
P.O. Box 1492
Washington, DC 20013
703-522-3332

The staff at the Educational Testing Service will provide parents of special junior and senior high school students with information about preparing for and taking SAT and achievement tests. Call any weekday between 8 A.M. and 4 P.M., EST.

Educational Testing Service
A.T.P. Services for Handicapped Students
CN6400
Princeton, NJ 08541–6400
609-734-3867

The HEATH Resource Center operates the National Clearinghouse on Postsecondary Education for Handicapped Individuals. The center encourages anyone to call, especially disabled students and their parents, educators, and administrators, for information on legislation, organizations willing to share specific information and advice, and training sessions and workshops. Fact sheets on accessibility, audiovisual materials, career development, financial aid, and rehabilitation programs are also available. They are especially strong on helping students plan ahead for vocational, college, or nonacademic programs. A staff member will help you any weekday between 9 A.M. and 5 P.M., EST.

Higher Education and the Handicapped
  (HEATH) Resource Center
1 Dupont Circle NW
Suite 670
Washington, DC 20036–1193
800-54-HEATH
202-833-4707 (In Washington, DC)

The Council for Exceptional Children (CEC) works on behalf of all children with special educational needs—gifted children, children with specific learning disabilities, and children who have emotional, cognitive, motor, visual, auditory, or communication handicaps—and is well known for championing the rights of special-needs individuals. The staff can provide: answers to any question you have about educational programs; helpful publications, including films and cassettes; conventions, workshops, and conferences; and special projects relating to multicultural education, parent-teacher relationships, paraprofessionals, and re-educating teacher educators. Call any weekday between the hours of 8 A.M. and 5 P.M., EST.

Council for Exceptional Children (CEC)
1920 Association Drive
Reston, VA 22091–1589
703-620-3660

o Sexual Abuse Prevention Programs See *Children and Child Care: Sexual Abuse.*

o Study Abroad

If you're interested in studying abroad, the Experiment in International Living is the place to call. This leader in the field of international education and training sponsors both B.A. and M.A. programs, all of which promote cross-cultural awareness and fulfillment of individual development potentials. Their goal is to promote peace and understanding through recognition of our positive interdependence. Single-semester programs are also available. Call any weekday between 8:30 A.M. and 4:30 P.M., EST.

The Experiment in International Living
Kipling Road
Brattleboro, VT 05301
800-451-4465

○ **Teaching Nuclear Issues** See *Environmental Issues: Nuclear Issues.*

○ **Women's Athletic Scholarships** See *Sports and Athletics: Women's Sports Foundation.*

● **EMPLOYMENT** See *Job Counseling.*

● **ENVIRONMENTAL ISSUES**

○ **Chemical Contamination**

Feminist theorist Dale Spender has called Rachel Carson one of the first "heretics" in the field of environmental science, and indeed, with the publication of *Silent Spring* in 1962, in which she detailed her fear that we are irresponsibly tampering with our environment—to our own detriment—she was calumniated by the chemical industry. The Rachel Carson Council has carried on to advance her philosophy by promoting public interest in and knowledge of our environment, by encouraging conservation measures, and by serving as a clearinghouse of information to scientists and interested consumers. If you have any question about the toxicity of pesticides, the effects of chemical contaminants and pesticides on human health and the environment, or the impact of chemical contamination on the economy, our government, and agricultural and industrial practices, call the council. Calls are taken every weekday between 9 A.M. and 5 P.M., EST.

Rachel Carson Council
8940 Jones Mill Rd.
Chevy Chase, MD 20815
202-652-1877

O Conservation See *Outdoors and Recreation: Conservation.*

O Hazardous Wastes

The Citizens Clearinghouse for Hazardous Wastes, Inc. (CCHW) is a nonprofit organization that provides citizen groups, individuals, and small municipalities with the information they need to understand and resolve their chemical-waste problems. CCHW's technical-assistance program is designed to assist people faced with technical questions on toxicity of chemicals, health effects resulting from exposure, how and where to test for chemicals, how to interpret health and environmental reports and data, and how to select the appropriate cleanup alternative. In addition, CCHW has a referral registry of consultants who can provide assistance beyond the expertise of the clearinghouse and a list of recognized experts who are available to discuss such topics as the regulations affecting waste disposal, remedial cleanup alternatives, how to conduct a health survey, disposal options, and public health risks. You can reach the clearinghouse between 9 A.M. and 5 P.M. on weekdays.

Citizens Clearinghouse for Hazardous Wastes,
    Inc.
P.O. Box 926
Arlington, VA 22216
703-276-7070

○ Nuclear Issues (See also *Health: Radiation Victims.*)

The Nuclear Information and Resource Service (NIRS) is a national clearinghouse and networking center for people concerned about nuclear issues. Antinuclear activists and concerned citizens are encouraged to call for up-to-date, reliable information, resources, and organizing assistance. Within NIRS's well-stocked library are files on every operating plant and reactor under construction, utility companies, and general nuclear issues. Information about teaching nuclear issues is also available, for a small cost. Call any weekday between 9 A.M. and 5:30 P.M., EST.

Nuclear Information and Resource Service
(NIRS)
1616 P Street NW
Washington, DC 20036
202-328-0002

○ Pesticides

The National Pesticide Telecommunications Network, formerly the National Pesticide Clearinghouse, provides a wealth of information on application and toxicity of pesticides. The staff can discuss pesticide contents and, for a nominal charge, will mail out scientific reports. The network is supported by the U.S. Environmental Protection Agency. The line is open around the clock, every day of the year.

National Pesticide Telecommunications
Network
Texas Tech University
Health Sciences Center
Lubbock, TX 79430
800-858-7378

The National Coalition against the Misuse of Pesticides (NCAMP) was formed as a broad coalition of health, environmental, labor, farm, consumer, and church groups, as well as individuals, who share common concerns about the potential hazards associated with pesticides. When you call, the staff will not only provide you with answers to your pesticide-related questions, it'll also offer advice on how to protect yourself and your family from the effects of pesticides and how to file a complaint if you have been exposed to a pesticide. A staff member will take your call any weekday between 9 A.M. and 5:30 P.M., EST.

National Coalition against the Misuse of
   Pesticides (NCAMP)
530 7th Street SE
Washington, DC 20003
202-543-5450

○ Pollution: General Information

The staff of the Office of Toxic Substances may be able to help you determine whether the waste floating in your stream is adding PCBs to the water. You can also get regulatory and technical guidance on the Toxic Substances Control Act requirements regarding public health and safety effects of new and existing chemicals and information on chemical hazards, risks, and instructional compliance aids. The line is staffed by trained professionals, weekdays from 8:30 A.M. to 5 P.M., EST.

Office of Toxic Substances
U.S. Environmental Protection Agency
401 M Street SW
Washington, DC 20460
800-424-9065
202-554-1404 (In Washington, DC)

If you have any question about water pollution, hazardous- and solid-waste disposal, air and noise pollution, pesticides, or radiation, a regional office of the U.S. Environmental Protection Agency is the first place to check. If the agency doesn't have the information you need, it will point you in the direction of someone who does. Agency offices are open on weekdays only.

Region 1 (CT, ME, MA, NH, RI, VT)
U.S. Environmental
    Protection Agency
John F. Kennedy Federal
    Building
Room 2203
Boston, MA 02203
617-223-7210
8:30 A.M. to 5 P.M., EST

Region 2 (NJ, NY, PR, VI)
U.S. Environmental
    Protection Agency
26 Federal Plaza, Room 900
New York, NY 10278
212-264-2525
8 A.M. to 6 P.M., EST

Region 3 (DE, DC, MD, PA, VA, WV)
U.S. Environmental
    Protection Agency
841 Chestnut Street
Philadelphia, PA 19107
215-597-9800
8 A.M. to 4:30 P.M., EST

Region 4 (AL, FL, GA, KY, MS, NC, SC, TN)
U.S. Environmental
    Protection Agency
345 Courtland Street NE
Atlanta, GA 30365
404-881-4727
8 A.M. to 5 P.M., EST

Region 5 (IL, IN, MI, MN, OH, WI)
U.S. Environmental
    Protection Agency
230 S. Dearborn Street
Chicago, IL 60604
312-353-2000
9 A.M. to 5 P.M., CST

Region 6 (LA, NM, OK, TX)
U.S. Environmental
    Protection Agency
1201 Elm Street
Dallas, TX 75270
214-767-2600
8 A.M. to 4:30 P.M., CST

Region 7 (IA, KS, MO, NE)
U.S. Environmental
    Protection Agency
726 Minnesota Avenue
Kansas City, KS 66101
913-236-2800
7:30 A.M. to 5 P.M., CST
For information on Dioxin-
    related issues in Missouri,
    dial **800-892-5009**. The
    line is open 24 hours a day.

Region 8 (CO, MT, ND, SD, UT, WY)
U.S. Environmental
    Protection Agency
999 18th Street, Suite 1300
Downtown Denver, CO
    80202
303-293-1603
8 A.M. to 5:30 P.M., MST

Region 9 (AZ, CA, GU, HI, NV, Samoa)
U.S. Environmental
  Protection Agency
215 Fremont Street
San Francisco, CA 94105
  415-974-8076
8:30 A.M. to 5 P.M., PST

Region 10 (AK, ID, OR, WA)
U.S. Environmental
  Protection Agency
1200 Sixth Ave.
Seattle, WA 98101
  206-442-5810
8 A.M. to 4:30 P.M., PST

○ **Toxic Substances and Birth Defects** See *Pregnancy, Birthing, and Family Planning: Toxic Substances and Birth Defects.*

F

• FABRICS AND TEXTILES

○ General Information

The Fashion Institute of Technology (FIT) is one of the most reliable and certainly one of the richest sources of information about the production and retailing of clothes in the country. If you've got a question about the history of fabrics, fashion trends, fashion designers, or anything else pertaining to clothes and fashion, this is the place to call. The library hours are variable, but you can be pretty sure that it will be open from 9 A.M. to 7 P.M., EST, Monday through Thursday, between 9 A.M. and 4 P.M. on Fridays during the summer. During the school year, the hours are likely to be 9 A.M. to 10 P.M., Monday through Thursday; 9 A.M. to 8 P.M., Fridays; noon to 5 P.M., Saturdays; and noon to 8 P.M., Sundays.

Fashion Institute of Technology (FIT)
227 W. 27th Street
New York, NY 10001
212-760-7590

○ Care and Handling

Wondering whether it's better to dry-clean or hand wash that new rayon dress you spent a fortune on? Call the experts at the American Apparel Manufacturers Association. They'll provide you with all the information you need about the care, handling, and performance record of various kinds of apparel. According to the director, the one question they can't answer is why manufacturers don't make more clothes in small sizes. Call weekdays between 9 A.M. and 5 P.M., EST.

American Apparel Manufacturers Association
Ann Lawrence, Educational Services Director
1611 N. Kent Street
Arlington, VA 22209
703-524-1864

o Cotton

Did you know that a high-protein concentrate derived from cotton seed can be, and is (!), used in baked goods, meat extenders, cereals, and soft drinks? These and other helpful bits of cotton history and trivia can be had from the National Cotton Council. The public relations officer will also provide you with information on cotton production, cotton marketing, and cotton landmarks. Teaching aids are available for a nominal cost. The council emphasizes that no care-and-handling information is available. Inquiries are accepted weekdays between 8:30 A.M. and 5 P.M., CST.

National Cotton Council of America
P.O. Box 12285
Memphis, TN 38182
901-274-9030

o Stain Removal

Just dripped cherry juice all over your new white shirt? Call the Stain Removal Hotline, an extension service of the Philadelphia College of Textiles and Science. The eminently knowledgeable and remarkably friendly staff will provide you with step-by-step instructions for removing the stain with potions made from ordinary household solutions (try a 50-50 mix of rubbing alcohol and tap water on the cherry stains—they'll come right out). However, the Stain Removal Center will not accept garments to identify stains. The hotline staff can provide you with general information about fabric care and handling. If you have a question about a "big ticket" item such as carpeting or upholstery, the staff will help you determine what type of fabric or textile is best suited for your needs. Call any weekday between 9 A.M. and 4 P.M., EST.

Stain Removal Hotline
Philadelphia College of Textiles and Science
School House Lane and Henry Avenue
Philadelphia, PA 19144
215-951-2757

● **FAMILY ECONOMICS** See *Personal Finances: Family Economics.*

● **FAMILY PLANNING** See *Pregnancy, Birthing, and Family Planning: Family Planning.*

● **FINDING LONG-LOST FRIENDS AND RELATIVES**

○ **Children** See *Children and Child Care: Missing and Exploited Children; Children and Child Care: Runaways.*

○ **Friends' Locator Service**

There are those of us who will go out of our way to avoid old friends, but there are others, nostomaniacs and worse, who will go out of their way to *find* old friends. Friend Finders International, founded by Herbert V. Farmer, a veteran with a longing to see fellow POWs from World War II, will help. An initial search via his computers, which at present can hold about thirty million names, costs $10; you're charged $10 more if the person you're looking for is found. All information is confidential. (By the way, if—heaven forfend—Friend Finders calls one day to say that someone is looking for you, it's up to you, not the seeker, to determine whether you want to be found.) The lines are open 24 hours a day, seven days a week.

Friend Finders International
314 Lloyd Building
Seattle, WA 98101
800-FINDERS

○ Genealogical Searches

The American Archives Association will engage in forensic genealogy to identify and locate missing and unknown heirs to estates. A percentage fee is levied for successful searches. For more information, call any weekday between 8:30 A.M. and 4:30 P.M., EST.

American Archives Association
1350 New York Avenue NW
Washington, DC 20005
202-737-6090

○ Tracing Family Trees

Although the staff at the National Archives will not engage in in-depth research, they will provide you with general information about genealogy and give you tips on hunting down your family roots. If your family has been in this country a long time, the staff may encourage you to visit the library itself: the coffers contain, among other choice bits, ship passenger records from 1820, military records from the Revolutionary War, and census forms from 1790 to 1900. A staff member will answer your inquiries every weekday from 8:45 A.M. to 5:15 P.M., EST.

National Archives and Records Administration
Reference Service Branch
Washington, DC 20408
202-523-3218

● **FOOD**   See *Diet and Nutrition.*

G

• GARDENS AND GARDENING

○ Gardening Books

The Horticulture Society of New York is a research-oriented facility and, as such, will not provide you with information about caring for your house plants or garden, but it will supply you with as much information as they have about relevant books and other printed material that might be useful. The society can also direct you to other sources of information. It answers calls from 9 A.M. to 5 P.M., EST, on Mondays, Tuesdays, Thursdays, and Fridays and from noon to 7 P.M. on Wednesdays.

Horticulture Society of New York
128 W. 58th Street
New York, NY 10019
212-757-0915

○ Lawn Care

Whether or not you use Scott's lawn-care products, the staff welcomes your calls about grass seed, fertilizer, and insect and weed controls. By calling this number, you can learn, for example, when and how to plant grass seed and fertilize your lawn and how to mow your lawn for optimum results. Calls are accepted weekdays from 9 A.M. to noon and from 12:30 P.M. to 5 P.M., EST.

Scott Lawn Hotline
O. M. Scott & Son
Marysville, OH 43041
800-543-TURF

○ **Maintenance** (See also *Information Centers: General.*)

What time of year should you plant the iris? Which ground cover is best for your property? What is the correct way to prune a hedge? How do you get rid of scale or mealybug on your house plants? Three experts at the famous Bronx Botanical Garden are on hand to answer your questions about indoor and outdoor plants, weekdays 10 A.M. to 4 P.M., EST.

Green Line
New York Botanical Garden
Bronx, NY 10458
212-220-8681

○ **Pests**

Mr. Louis Sorkin, an expert in arthropods at the American Museum of Natural History, will be happy to answer any questions you have about ants, spiders, lobsters, and other arthropods. If you have an insect that you cannot identify, you may actually mail it to Mr. Sorkin, and he will be glad to tell you what it is and to furnish its natural history. However, if insects are not your hobby, but the bane of your existence, Mr. Sorkin, who is a consultant on pest control, will be happy to discuss the finer points of eliminating your problem. Mr. Sorkin is in his office weekdays from 2:30 P.M. to 5 P.M., EST.

Louis Sorkin
American Museum of Natural History
81st Street and Central Park West
New York, NY 10024
212-873-1300, ext. **623**

○ **Roses**

Dog-eared roses embarrassing you and your neighbors? Call the American Rose Society. The society will answer any question you have about roses, rose diseases, and coping strategies. General information about horticulture and landscape design is also available. Call any weekday between 8:30 A.M. and 4:30 P.M., EST.

American Rose Society Library
P.O. Box 30,000
Shreveport, LA 71130
318-938-5402

● **GAYS AND LESBIANS** See *Lesbians and Gays.*

● **GENEALOGY** See *Finding Long-Lost Friends and Relatives.*

H

• HAIR AND SKIN CARE

○ Hair

The trained staff at Clairol will try to provide you with a satisfactory answer about any hair-care product you're interested in, be it Clairol's or a competing brand's. The staff will also give you expert advice on hair care, hair coloring, and remedial measures. When I asked if that meant that I could call and find out how I could get the crazy green out of my hair that I had just put in, the woman I was speaking to told me that yes, indeed she could help me, provided that I knew the brand name of the dye I had used. I was impressed. Clairol accepts calls weekdays between 8:30 A.M. and 8 P.M., EST.

Clairol Hotline
Clairol, Inc.
345 Park Avenue
New York, NY 10154
800-223-5800
212-644-2990 (Collect)

○ Skin

The staff at the Skin Care Hotline will answer your questions about facials, cosmetics, and skin-care programs and will help you to determine if a consultation with a dermatologist is recommended. The skin-care specialists will answer your inquiries weekdays from 9 A.M. to 5 P.M., CST.

Skin Care Hotline
3012 Armstrong Street
Dallas, TX 75205
800-527-5448
214-526-0760 (In Dallas)

● **HANDICAPPED** See *Health: Physical Handicaps.*

○ **Books** See *Reading and Writing: Books for the Blind and Physically Handicapped.*

○ **Children** See *Education: Resources for the Learning Disabled and Handicapped.*

○ **Computers** See *Computers: Special Education Systems.*

○ **Employment** See *Business: Accommodating the Handicapped.*

● **HEALTH**

○ **Abortion** See *Pregnancy, Birthing, and Family Planning: Abortion.*

○ **AIDS** (See also *Information Centers: Lesbians and Gays.*)

The experts at this hotline offer basic information to callers about acquired immune deficiency syndrome (AIDS), including symptoms, possible causes, and recommended preventive measures. Referrals to specialists are also available. Call weekdays between 3 P.M. and 9 P.M., EST.

National Gay Task Force Crisisline
80 Fifth Avenue
New York, NY 10011
800-221-7044
212-807-6016 (In New York, Alaska, and
    Hawaii)

The Public Health Service AIDS Information Hotline is a prerecorded and detailed message that provides information to the public about the prevention and spread of AIDS. The line is open 24 hours a day.

Public Health Service AIDS Information
Hotline
Centers for Disease Control
1600 Clifton Road NE
Atlanta, GA 30333
800-342-AIDS
If you would like more information or would like to speak to a trained counselor, dial **800-447-AIDS.**

O **Alcoholism**   (See also *Business: Alcohol Rehabilitation Programs.*)

Alcoholics Anonymous (A.A.) is an international fellowship of women and men who have or have had a drinking problem. It is nonprofessional, self-supporting, nondenominational, multiracial, and apolitical. Membership is open to anyone who wants to do something about her or his drinking problem. For information on the chapter nearest you or for information on how to develop a self-help program for other types of addicts using A.A. methods, call the number listed below. They're open weekdays from 9 A.M. to 5 P.M., EST.

A.A. World Services Office
468 Park Avenue South
New York, NY 10016
212-686-1100

Alcoholism is now recognized as a disease that affects the whole family, and Al-Anon is a fellowship that tries to meet and alleviate the problems of the millions of people—lovers, sisters, brothers, spouses, children, friends, and parents—who are affected by close contact with an alcoholic. If you have a question about an alcohol-related problem in your home, Al-Anon will answer your question, send you free literature, and/or refer you to other sources of information and help. Referrals are available to those interested in joining a group, as is information on starting a new group. If you have a problem with your Al-Anon group, you can explain the situation to the advisor at this number. A special support program called Alateen is available for teenagers. The office is open every weekday between 9 A.M. and 5 P.M., EST.

Al-Anon
1 Park Avenue, 2d Floor
New York, NY 10016
212-683-1771

The staff at the National Clearinghouse for Alcohol Information will provide you with general information on alcohol-related problems and programs. Referrals to treatment centers are also available; over-the-phone counseling is not. Call any weekday between 8:30 A.M. and 5 P.M., EST.

National Clearinghouse for Alcohol
  Information
P.O. Box 2345
Rockville, MD 20852
301-468-2600

○ Allergies and Respiratory Diseases

The experts at the National Asthma Center, a renowned research center, answer questions about the early detection, care, and prevention of asthma, emphysema, chronic bronchitis, juvenile rheumatoid arthritis, and other respiratory and immune-system disorders. If they don't have the answer, they'll check with another respiratory specialist and get back to you, usually within 24 hours. The line is open 24 hours a day, seven days a week.

Lung Line
National Jewish Hospital and Research Center
National Asthma Center
3800 E. Colfax Avenue
Denver, CO 80206
800-222-LUNG
303-398-1477 (In Colorado)

The American Academy of Allergy and Immunology will provide general information to allergy sufferers and the general public. Referrals to allergists and other specialists are also available. The staff can also provide a list of summer camps that cater to children with allergies. Free publications will be sent on request. Call weekdays between 8:30 A.M. and 5 P.M., CST.

The American Academy of Allergy and
  Immunology
611 E. Wells Street
Milwaukee, WI 53202
414-272-6071

Emphysema Anonymous is a nationwide organization that provides educational information and mutual assistance to anyone suffering upper-respiratory insufficiencies. Many local chapters maintain a "loan closet" of breathing equipment which may be borrowed for ninety days, and some provide 24-hour counseling services for emphysema sufferers and their families. Check your local telephone directory for the number of the chapter nearest you; if you are unable to locate one, call the number listed below. The staff will be happy to help weekdays between 8 A.M. and 5 P.M., EST. After hours, you may leave a message with the service.

Emphysema Anonymous
P.O. Box 66
Fort Myers, FL 33902
813-334-4226

O Alzheimer's Disease

The Physicians Center for Gerontology is an information center emanating from a private physicians' center, that will field inquiries from the general public and health-care professionals about Alzheimer's disease. They cannot make referrals to support groups or physicians. Call weekdays between 7:30 A.M. and 4 P.M., CST.

The Physicians Center for Gerontology
2447 N. Southport
Chicago, IL 60614
312-327-5500

The Alzheimer's Disease and Related Disorders Association will provide information about publications which refer to or explain Alzheimer's disease and related disorders. Referrals to local chapters and support groups are also available. Call any weekday between 9 A.M. and 5:30 P.M., CST. After 5:30 P.M., an answering machine will record your message; someone will get back to you the next morning.

Alzheimer's Disease and Related Disorders
    Association
360 N. Michigan Avenue
Chicago, IL 60601
800-621-0379
800-572-6037 (In Illinois)

O Anorexia and Bulimia

As Susie Orhbach has written, fat (or the lack thereof) is a feminist issue: studies indicate that over 20 percent of young women between the ages of 10 and 25 years have trouble fitting themselves into the emaciated model of twentieth-century femininity they've been trained to aspire to. The staff at BASH (Bulimia Anorexia Self-Help) will counsel women and men who want help accepting their own physicality and will discuss candidly and confidentially fears of obesity, dieting, and personality changes. Advice is also offered to concerned parents. Referrals to counseling centers, physicians, and self-help groups are available. Call on weekdays between 8:30 A.M. and 5 P.M., CST.

BASH
1027 Bellevue Avenue
St. Louis, MO 63117
800-BASH-STL
314-991-BASH (In Missouri)

O Arthritis

Want to know what research is taking place on your form of arthritis? How others similarly afflicted cope? This health-education service, emanating from a private doctor's office, is savvy on the latest thinking regarding arthritis, although it's not equipped to give referrals on a national basis. The center is staffed weekdays from 9 A.M. to 5 P.M., EST.

Arthritis Medical Center
901 S.E. 17th Street
Suite 200
Fort Lauderdale, FL 33316
800-327-3027
305-522-5662 (In Florida)

O Athletic Injuries See *Sports and Athletics: Sports Medicine; Sports and Athletics: Women's Sports Foundation.*

O Blindness and Visual Impairments (See also *Reading and Writing: Books for the Blind and Physically Handicapped.*)

The Jewish Guild for the Blind is a not-for-profit, nonsectarian agency serving blind, visually impaired, and multidisabled individuals. The guild can confidently boast that it serves all the needs of the visually handicapped and will provide you with information on, among other things, rehabilitation, job placement, special education programs, and day programs. The guild's cassette library is the largest circulator of taped best-sellers and other books for the blind in the world. A guild member will be happy to help you any weekday between 9 A.M. and 5 P.M., EST.

The Jewish Guild for the Blind
15 W. 65th Street
New York, NY 10023
212-595-2000

The "Washington Connection" is a toll-free, after-hours taped message, sponsored by the American Council of the Blind. It gives a quick overview of current legislation affecting the blind and physically handicapped, along with suggestions on whom to contact to make your opinion known. Updates are almost weekly. The message runs weekdays from 6 P.M. to 9 A.M., EST, and on weekends it runs around the clock.

"Washington Connection"
1211 Connecticut Avenue NW
Suite 506
Washington, DC 20036
800-424-8666
202-466-4855 (In Washington, DC, Alaska, and
    Hawaii)

The experts at the National Retinitis Pigmentosa Foundation will answer your questions about genetics, current research, and retina-donor programs. The local number connects callers with a specialist who can answer questions regarding retinitis pigmentosa. Call any weekday between 8:30 A.M. and 5 P.M., EST.

National Retinitis Pigmentosa Foundation
8333 Mindale Circle
Baltimore, MD 21207
800-638-2300
301-655-1011

○ Cancer

If you have any question about cancer, an accurate, personalized answer is available from the Cancer Information Service, a program of the National Cancer Institute. The staff can also provide you with information about treatment options, prevention, and coping strategies. Publications are available (free) as are referrals to counseling centers. Hours vary, but, in general, calls are answered between 8 A.M. and midnight, seven days a week. Most of the numbers have backup numbers with recorded messages available after hours. Spanish-speaking staff members are available to callers from the following areas (daytime hours only): California (area codes 213, 714, 619, 805), Florida, Georgia, Illinois, northern New Jersey, New York City, and Texas.

Cancer Information Service
National Cancer Institute
Bethesda, MD 20205
800-4-CANCER
202-636-5700 (In Washington, DC, suburbs in
   Maryland and Virginia)
808-524-1234 (In Oahu, HI; neighbor islands
   call collect)
800-638-6070 (In Alaska)

The staff at the American Medical Center provides the latest information on cancer causes, prevention, methods of detection and diagnosis, treatment and treatment facilities, rehabilitation, and counseling services. Calls are answered by staff members weekdays between 8 A.M. and 5 P.M., MST; a prerecorded message will greet you after hours.

American Medical Center
Cancer Research Center
1600 Pierce
Denver, CO 80214
800-525-3777

The Candlelighters Childhood Cancer Foundation is a parent support group that will research medical information on the latest treatments for juvenile cancer for parents or other interested persons. A list of local chapters and a list of camps for children with cancer are available. The organization cannot make referrals. Call any weekday between 9 A.M. and 5 P.M., EST.

The Candlelighters Childhood Cancer
   Foundation
2025 Eye Street NW
Suite 1011
Washington, DC 20006
202-659-5136

The Corporate Angel Network, managed by the American Cancer Society, provides free airplane transportation to and from recognized treatment facilities, using empty seats on routine corporate flights. Patients must be able to walk and must not need special support services. A trained volunteer will answer your questions about the service any weekday between 8:30 A.M. and 4:30 P.M., EST.

The Corporate Angel Network, Inc.
Building One
Westchester County Airport
White Plains, NY 10604
914-328-1313

o Cerebral Palsy

The experts at the United Cerebral Palsy Association will supply you with information about guidance programs for cerebral palsy sufferers. They can also provide general information to families, friends, and the interested public about the cause and treatment of cerebral palsy. The phone is answered weekdays between 8:45 A.M. and 4:45 P.M., EST.

United Cerebral Palsy Association, Inc.
66 E. 34th Street
New York, NY 10016
212-481-6300

o Cystic Fibrosis

In addition to offering general information on cystic fibrosis, the staff at the Cystic Fibrosis Foundation provides referrals to accredited care centers. Literature is also available, as is information about the latest research. If you require more detailed information than the foundation can provide, a staff member will point you in the right direction. Call any weekday between 8:30 A.M. and 5 P.M., EST.

Cystic Fibrosis Foundation
6000 Executive Boulevard
Rockville, MD 20852
800-FIGHT-CF
301-881-9130 (In Maryland)

o DES

DES Action National is a nonprofit consumer group dedicated to informing the public and health professionals about the effects of diethylstilbestrol (DES) exposure and what can be done about it. The staffer who answers the phone can refer you to a physician in your area familiar with DES and the problems it causes, give you the name and address of a support group in your area, and direct you to a screening center if you are not sure whether you have been affected. They will also advise you of the known effects of DES in daughters and sons of mothers who took DES during pregnancy.

DES Action National
Long Island Jewish Medical Center
New Hyde Park, NY 11040
(9 A.M. to 4 P.M., EST, Tuesday and Thursday)
516-775-3450

DES Action National
2845 24th Street
San Francisco, CA 94110
(10 A.M. to 5 P.M., PST, weekdays) **415-826-5060**

O Diabetes

The staff of the American Diabetes Association will provide callers with information about diabetes, its symptoms, and possible treatment procedures. Physician referrals, support-group assistance information, and information on camps that cater to children with diabetes are also available. Call weekdays between 9 A.M. and 5 P.M., EST. After hours, leave a message on the answering machine; someone will get back to you the next working day.

American Diabetes Association
2 Park Avenue
New York, NY 10016
800-227-6776
800-232-3427
212-683-7444 (In New York)

The staff at the Juvenile Diabetes Foundation will answer questions on juvenile diabetes and offer referrals to physicians and clinics. Publications are also available. Call any weekday between 9 A.M. and 5 P.M., EST.

International Hotline
Juvenile Diabetes Foundation
60 Madison Avenue
New York, NY 10010–1150
800-223-1138
212-889-7575 (In New York)

O Digestive Disorders

The staff at Gutline—an aptly named hotline—will answer any questions you have about digestive diseases and disorders, including hemorrhoids, ulcers, diverticulosis, or irritable bowel syndrome. No diagnoses are offered over the phone, but they will refer you to a gastroenterologist if desired. The staff fields inquiries on Tuesdays between 7:30 P.M. and 9 P.M., EST.

Gutline
American Digestive Disease Society
7720 Wisconsin Avenue
Bethesda, MD 20814
301-652-9293

o Down Syndrome

The staff at the National Down Syndrome Society will provide you with general information on Down syndrome. Referrals to local programs for the newborn are also available. Call any weekday between 9 A.M. and 5 P.M., EST. After hours, leave a message on the answering machine.

National Down Syndrome Society Hotline
National Down Syndrome Society
70 W. 40th Street
New York, NY 10018
800-221-4602
212-460-9330 (In New York)

o Drug Abuse

The specialists at the National Cocaine Hotline—an information and crisis counseling center—can provide you with answers to questions about the health risks of cocaine and can refer callers to physicians or treatment centers nearest their homes. Immediate counseling to users and their friends and families is also available. By the way, when you call, you can feel confident that you're talking to an expert: 50 percent of the staff members were formerly drug dependent. Upon request, a free packet of information will be sent to you. Some information on other frequently misused drugs is also available. The phone is answered 24 hours a day, every day of the year.

National Cocaine Hotline
Fair Oaks Hospital
19 Prospect Street
Summit, NJ 07901
800-COCAINE

The people at PRIDE, a nonprofit educational organization founded and staffed by Georgia State University, furnish information on available drug programs and keep a list of drug and alcohol treatment centers by city and state. They also sell books and films on drug abuse prevention and offer tips on coordinating a drug awareness program in your school or community. Weekdays from 9 A.M. to 5 P.M., EST, a staff member will answer your questions directly; at all other times, provided you have a Touch-tone phone, you may listen to a selection of tapes providing various kinds of drug information.

Parents' Resource Institute for Drug Education
  (PRIDE)
100 Edgewood Avenue
Suite 1216
Atlanta, GA 30303
800-241-7946
800-282-4241 (In Georgia, except Atlanta)
404-658-2548 (In Atlanta)

The National Institute on Drug Abuse Prevention was established to provide schools, parent groups, business and industry, and national organizations with information and technical assistance on developing drug abuse prevention activities. They do not, however, provide crisis counseling, intervention-treatment referrals, information on the pharmacology of drugs, or information on the criminal aspects of selling illicit drugs. The staff is ready to answer your questions weekdays between 9 A.M. and 6 P.M., EST.

National Institute on Drug Abuse Prevention
5600 Fishers Lane
Rockville, MD 20857
800-638-2045
301-443-2450 (In Washington, DC)

The main goal of the National Federation of Parents for Drug-Free Youth is to provide parents with referrals to support groups and centers for drug abuse and juvenile alcohol treatment. Basic information about juvenile addiction is also available. Call weekdays between 9 A.M. and 5 P.M., EST.

National Federation of Parents for Drug-Free
  Youth
1820 Franwall Avenue
Suite 16
Silver Spring, MD 20902
800-554-KIDS
301-649-7100 (In Maryland)

The Alcohol and Drug Hotline is a national service that operates from Doctor's Hospital in Worcester, Massachusetts; it provides preliminary consultation and referral for problem drinkers and drug abusers. Hotline calls are taken by staff members who are required to complete extensive training before being allowed to operate the phones. The line is open 24 hours a day.

Alcohol and Drug Hotline
107 Lincoln Street
Worcester, MA 01605
800-252-6465

o Drug Information

If you're wondering about the possible side effects of those horse capsules your doctor prescribed for you, call the Food and Drug Administration's Center for Drugs and Biologics. They'll provide you with all the information they have on that drug, its side effects, and its labeling requirements. The center can also give you information about areas of research on specific prescription drugs and "problem" drugs. Service agents can take your calls on weekdays between 9 A.M. and 4 P.M., EST.

Food and Drug Administration
Center for Drugs and Biologics
5600 Fishers Lane
Room 15B32
Rockville, MD 20857
301-443-1016

The National Association of Retail Druggists, representing over 30,000 independent pharmacy owners, will happily provide callers with information on prescription drugs, poison control, mail-order drug frauds, veterinary drugs, drug labeling and package inserts, effective storage measures, and almost any other area of pharmacopeia. Information on employment opportunities in retail pharmacy is also available, as are referrals to other sources of information. The office is open weekdays from 9 A.M. to 5 P.M., EST.

National Association of Retail Druggists
205 Daingerfield Road
Alexandria, VA 22314
703-683-8200

o **Dyslexia**   See *Education: Resources for the Learning Disabled and Handicapped.*

o Emergency Services

The numbers listed for Medic Alert are not hotline numbers; rather, they will get you in touch with the business offices of a nonprofit organization with information that might—if you're a member—save your life. By making available through their office previously registered information describing diagnosis, treatment, or necessary handling, Medic Alert intercedes for persons when they cannot speak for themselves. Members register such conditions as diabetes, asthma, Alzheimer's disease, and retardation, as well as wishes regarding donation of organs on death. A call to this number will fetch information on the service as well as an application and a questionnaire, but membership is required for further phone contact. One-time fees start at $15, depending on the type of identification jewelry ordered. The phone is answered 24 hours a day, every day of the year.

Medic Alert
P.O. Box 95381–1000
2323 Colorado
Turlock, CA 95380
800-344-3226
800-468-1020 (In California)
209-668-3333 (Turlock area)

Lifeline, a personal emergency system, is a practical, inexpensive, 24-hour system available to the disabled who want to live in their homes. This is how it works: a wireless transmitter which can be carried in a pocket or attached to clothing sends, when triggered, a message to a communicator in a home phone. The phone then automatically dials a hospital or other community agency where monitored equipment has been set up. The response center has an information card for each Lifeline user, listing medical conditions and people to be called in an emergency. These are backed up by community service providers such as ambulance services and police. For more information, call any weekday from 8:30 A.M. to 5:30 P.M., EST.

Lifeline Systems, Inc.
1 Arsenal Marketplace
Watertown, MA 02172
800-451-0525
617-923-4141

○ **Endometriosis** See *Health: Reproductive Health; Pregnancy, Birthing, and Family Planning: General Information.*

○ Epilepsy

The Epilepsy Foundation of America is committed to the prevention and control of epilepsy and to improving the lives of people who suffer from epilepsy. Toward this goal, various educational, advocacy, and research programs are sponsored. When you call, a staff member will provide you with information, referrals, or counseling as you wish. The names and addresses of self-help groups and parent groups are also available here, as is information on medical, financial, and legal assistance. Check your telephone directory for the nearest EFA affiliate. If you can't find an affiliate near you, call the national office at the number listed below. That office is open every weekday between 9 A.M. and 5 P.M., EST.

Epilepsy Foundation of America
4351 Garden City Drive
Landover, MD 20785
301-459-3700

○ Growth Problems

Whether or not a growth problem can be treated, stunted children and their families often benefit from participation in organizations that provide emotional support and technical information. The staff at the Human Growth Foundation will provide interested parties with information about parent education, support groups, and current pituitary gland research. Calls are accepted on weekdays between 9 A.M. and 5 P.M., EST.

Human Growth Foundation
4607 Davidson Drive
Chevy Chase, MD 20815
301-656-7540

o Hansen's Disease (Leprosy)

The American Leprosy Mission is perhaps the most reliable source around for information on Hansen's disease. Questions are accepted from both the layperson and the medical professional weekdays between 8:30 A.M. and 4:30 P.M., EST.

American Leprosy Missions
1 Broadway
Elmwood Park, NJ 07407
800-543-3131
201-794-8650 (In New Jersey, Alaska, and
   Hawaii)

o Health Information Advisory

The National Health Information Clearinghouse (NHIC) is a central source of information and referral for all kinds of health questions. When you call, the information specialist determines which of the resources in NHIC's computer data base (including government agencies, support groups, professional societies, and other health-related organizations) can best answer your inquiry. Your question is then forwarded to that agency, which responds to you directly. NHIC is *not* able to conduct in-depth research, perform computerized literature searches, give medical advice, diagnose diseases, or recommend health-care providers. Upon request, NHIC will send you free publications on nutrition and health. Call any weekday between 8:30 A.M. and 5 P.M., EST.

National Health Information Clearinghouse
P.O. Box 1133
Washington, DC 20013–1133
800-336-4797
703-522-2590 (In Virginia)

o Health Information Library   See *Health Information Library, p. 124.*

o Hearing and Speech Disorders

The Better Hearing Institute is a private nonprofit organization that will send you information on better hearing and the prevention of deafness. The institute also provides a referral service but will not, in general, discuss hearing problems over the phone. This line is open weekdays from 9 A.M. to 5 P.M., EST.

Hearing Helpline
Better Hearing Institute
P.O. Box 1840
Washington, DC 20013
800-424-8576
202-638-7577 (In Washington, DC)

The National Hearing Aid Helpline is perhaps the best place to go for information on hearing aids and hearing-aid specialists certified by the National Hearing Aid Society. When you call, the staff member will answer your questions and refer you to a specialist if needed. Inquiries are accepted weekdays between 9 A.M. and 5 P.M., EST.

National Hearing Aid Helpline
National Hearing Aid Society
20361 Middlebelt
Lavonia, MI 48152
800-521-5247
313-478-2610 (In Michigan)

The National Association for Hearing and Speech Action Line offers information on hearing and speech problems and distributes materials on pathologists and audiologists certified by the American Speech-Language-Hearing Association. Information on hearing aids and other topics related to hearing and speech is also available here. The phone is answered weekdays between 8:30 A.M. and 5 P.M., EST.

National Association for Hearing and Speech
  Action Line
10801 Rockville Pike
Rockville, MD 20852
800-638-8255
301-897-8682 (In Maryland, Alaska, and Hawaii;
  call collect)

The National Association of the Deaf is an organization of hearing-impaired and deaf people; professionals, parents, and state associations will provide you with information about rehabilitation programs, family and personal counseling, education, employment, and discrimination. The association, which also serves as a clearinghouse on the deaf, makes some legal information available. Referrals to local treatment centers are available. Inquiries are accepted weekdays between 8:45 A.M. and 5 P.M., EST.

National Association of the Deaf
814 Thayer Avenue
Silver Spring, MD 20910
301-587-1788

The National Crisis Center for the Deaf is a nationwide, 24-hour service that provides immediate emergency aid, usually in the form of an ambulance or police officer, to the deaf. It is for use only by deaf and hearing-impaired people.

National Crisis Center for the Deaf
P.O. Box 484
University of Virginia Hospital
Charlottesville, VA 22908
800-446-9876
800-552-3723 (In Virginia)

o Heart Disease

The New York affiliate of the American Heart Association has established a Nutrition Counseling Referral Service that will provide the name and address of a registered dietitian (R.D.) in New York City who will answer your questions about saturated fat, cholesterol, sodium, sugar, calories, and other gastronomical delights that advance one's propensity for heart disease. These certified nutritionists (all of whom specialize in cardiovascular concerns) not only will help prepare a healthful diet prescription for you but also will offer you advice on food budgeting, shopping, and preparation. Both the New York office and the registered dietitian should be able to give you information about insurance coverage for such consultations. Upon request, free publications will be sent. If you're interested in finding out more about the lean life, first try your local affiliate of the American Heart Association (it should be listed in the phone directory); if they have not yet established a similar program and are unfamiliar with any in your area, call the New York office. The staff there may be able to refer you. Staff members answer your calls weekdays between 8:30 A.M. and 5 P.M., EST.

American Heart Association
New York City Affiliate
205 E. 42d Street
New York, NY 10017
212-661-5335

The staff at Heartlife will provide you with answers to your questions about heart diseases and pacemakers. They also distribute a quarterly periodical titled *Pulse* (what else?) and will mail subscriber information to you on request. Call weekdays from 9 A.M. to 4 P.M., EST. After hours, an answering service will record your message.

Heartlife
P.O. Box 54305
Atlanta, GA 30308
800-241-6993
404-523-0826 (In Georgia)

○ Hemophilia

The trained staff at the National Hemophilia Foundation will provide callers with information about hemophilia, its diagnosis, and its treatment. They are especially strong on pain-control information and medical information for hemophiliac athletes. Referrals to treatment centers and local chapters are also available, as is information on summer camps for kids. The staff can also provide information about AIDS and hemophilia. Call any weekday between 9 A.M. and 5 P.M., EST.

National Hemophilia Foundation
110 Greene Street, Room 406
New York, NY 10012
212-219-8180

○ High Blood Pressure

If you have any question regarding high blood pressure, be it about detection, diagnosis, medication, or home measuring devices, call the High Blood Pressure Information Center. The center will provide you with quick answers and mail you a pamphlet or two to back it up. A staff member will answer your questions any weekday between 8:30 A.M. and 5 P.M., EST.

High Blood Pressure Information Center
120/80 National Institute of Health
Bethesda, MD 20205
301-496-1809

○ Homeopathy

Homeopathy is a medical specialty that treats persons through the use of natural medicines that stimulate a person's own healing processes and avoid potentially harmful side effects. When you call the National Center for Homeopathy, a staff member will answer your questions about homeopathic medicine and refer you to homeopathic practitioners in your area. Call any weekday between 9 A.M. and 5 P.M., EST.

National Center for Homeopathy
1500 Massachusetts Avenue NW
Washington, DC 20005
202-223-6182

The staff at the American Holistic Medical Association will provide you with referrals to holistic medical practitioners in your area and will offer an overview of their specialties. Information on nutritional guides and bibliographies is also available. Call weekdays between 8:30 A.M. and 5 P.M., EST.

American Holistic Medical Association
6932 Little River Turnpike
Suite A
Annandale, VA 22003
703-642-5880

○ Hospital Care

The staff on the referral line at the Shriners Hospital for Crippled Children will provide information on free hospital care available to children under 18 years of age who need orthopedic care or burn treatment. To find out if you're eligible, call any weekday between 8 A.M. and 5 P.M., EST.

Shriners Hospital for Crippled Children
  Referral Line
P.O. Box 25356
Tampa, FL 33622
800-237-5055
800-282-9161 (In Florida)

In 1946, Congress passed a law which gave hospitals and other health facilities money for construction and modernization. In return, the facilities which received these Hill-Burton funds agree to (1) provide a reasonable volume of services to persons unable to pay, and (2) make their services available to all persons residing in the facility's area. To find out more about the Hill-Burton program and to obtain information about your eligibility, leave your name, address, and a brief message on the answering machine. (The machine is set to record your calls 24 hours a day.) A staff member will return your call.

Hill-Burton Hospital Free Care
Rockville, MD 20857
800-638-0742
800-492-0359 (In Maryland)

o Hysterectomy

If you're wondering whether the hysterectomy your doctor has advised is the appropriate alternative, call the HERS Foundation. A trained staff member will counsel you as to your options and suggest questions to take back to your doctor. If you have already had a hysterectomy and would like some help coping with the aftereffects, a member of the HERS Foundation can help. (A newsletter and publications are also available.) Call any weekday between 9 A.M. and 5 P.M., EST; after hours, you may leave a message on the answering machine and someone will get back to you within 24 hours. If your problem is urgent, indicate that on the machine, and someone will get back to you the same evening.

Hysterectomy Educational Resources and
   Services Foundation (HERS)
422 Bryn Mawr Avenue
Bala Cynwyd, PA 19004
215-667-7757

o Incontinence

The Simon Foundation, a not-for-profit agency founded by Cheryle B. Gartley, author of *Managing Incontinence: A Guide to Living with the Loss of Urinary Control,* is dedicated to removing the social stigma associated with incontinence. When you call, a member of the staff will supply you with information about services and self-help groups available to sufferers, their families, and their friends and will review laws and rules which may affect the incontinent. The newsletter *The Informer* will be sent to you upon request. Call any weekday between 9 A.M. and 5 P.M., CST.

The Simon Foundation
P.O. Box 815
Wilmette, IL 60091
800-23-SIMON
312-864-3913 (In Illinois)

HIP, Inc., is a self-help and patient advocacy group organized to assist Americans and Canadians who have bladder-control problems. It functions as a clearinghouse of information and services both for consumers, their families, and friends and for medical, nursing, and social service professionals. HIP's newsletter, published quarterly, gives the results of their product testers' evaluations of specially designed garments and devices and offers a listing of helpful organizations and services. HIP is most proud of their recently released audiocassette that, believe it or not, coaches you through pelvic-floor exercises that help maintain continence. A small booklet accompanies the tape and further explains the exercises. Referrals are also available. For more information, call any weekday between 8:30 A.M. and 5 P.M., EST.

Help for Incontinent People (HIP)
P.O. Box 544
Union, SC 29379
803-585-8789

If you are 55 or older and want some answers about incontinence, the Continence Clinic may be able to help. Although not equipped to make referrals, the clinic will field inquiries (their area of concentration is stress incontinence) and provide you with helpful information about bladder control. Call any weekday between 7:30 A.M. and 4 P.M., CST.

Continence Clinic
Physicians Center for Gerontology
2447 N. Southport
Chicago, IL 60614
312-327-5500

The Continence Restored program, which emanates from a private urologist's office, is designed to help men whose urinary incontinence is related to sexual dysfunction or vice versa. Presently, the members of the program are working to establish a network of support groups around the country. If you'd like more information or have any inquiry related to the above, call any weekday between 9 A.M. and 5 P.M., EST.

Continence Restored
Dr. E. Douglas Whitehead
785 Park Avenue
New York, NY 10021
212-879-3131

The Harvard Geriatric Clinic is a university-based research center that provides both the lay public and scholars with information about incontinence and bladder control. Referrals are not available. Call on a weekday, anytime between 8 A.M. and 5 P.M., EST.

The Harvard Geriatric Clinic
Brigham and Women's Hospital
75 Francis Street
Boston, MA 02115
617-732-6844

O **Infertility** (See also *Pregnancy, Birthing, and Family Planning: Family Planning.*)

Couples troubled by infertility can call Resolve to receive immediate emotional support and expert information about the latest treatment for infertility. Referrals to specialists, therapists, and local chapters are also provided. General adoption information will also be supplied. Call any weekday from 9 A.M. to noon and from 1 P.M. to 4 P.M., EST.

Resolve National Phone Counseling Line
Resolve Inc.
P.O. Box 474
Belmont, MA 02178
617-484-2424

○ Insomnia

Haven't been to sleep since last Thursday? Call the Lenox Hill Hospital SleepLine. The SleepLine message, answered automatically by machine, offers instructions on how to fall asleep without using drugs. In fact, the SleepLine message is designed to help you fall asleep as you listen. Go ahead, try it—I hear it's a knockout! By the way, the SleepLine is available 24 hours a day, all year round.

SleepLine
Lenox Hill Hospital
Health Education Center
100 E. 77th Street
New York, NY 10021
212-772-7800

○ Kidney Diseases

If you suffer from any kind of kidney disease and are unable to pay the cost of treatment, contact the American Kidney Fund. The fund's staff will let you know if you are eligible for financial assistance and can also provide information on organ donations and kidney-related diseases. Call any week-day between 8 A.M. and 6 P.M., EST.

American Kidney Fund
7315 Wisconsin Avenue
Suite 203 East
Bethesda, MD 20814
800-638-8299
800-492-8361 (In Maryland)

○ Leukemia

The members of the Leukemia Society of America offer coun-seling and support to leukemia patients and their families. Referrals to physicians and treatment centers are also availa-ble. Call any weekday between 8 A.M. and 5 P.M., EST.

Leukemia Society of America
1625 Eye Street NW
Suite 923
Washington, DC 20006
202-223-2656

○ Maternal and Child Health (See also *Children and Child Care; Pregnancy, Birthing, and Family Planning: Maternal Health.*)

The staff of the National Clearinghouse for Maternal and Child Health will answer questions regarding genetics, develop-mental disabilities, and sickle cell anemia, among other things. If you desire more-detailed information such as statistical sur-veys, a staff member will tell you where to find what you need. Call any weekday between 8:30 A.M. and 5 P.M., EST.

National Clearinghouse for Maternal and Child
  Health
3520 Prospect Street NW
Ground Floor, Suite 1
Washington, DC 20057
202-625-8410

o **Menopause** See *Health: Women's Health Network; Pregnancy, Birthing, and Family Planning: General Information.*

o **Midwifery** See *Pregnancy, Birthing, and Family Planning: Midwifery.*

o Multiple Sclerosis

The trained staff at the National Multiple Sclerosis Society will provide any interested party with information about the cause, the cure, and the prevention of multiple sclerosis. Upon request, information about various patient services and public and professional educational programs will be provided. Your inquiries will be taken any weekday between the hours of 9 A.M. and 5 P.M., EST.

National Multiple Sclerosis Society
205 E. 42d Street
New York, NY 10017
212-986-3240

o Muscular Dystrophy

The Muscular Dystrophy Association will supply to people afflicted with muscular dystrophy, their family, and friends general information about the disease and about services for muscular dystrophy sufferers. Information about professional and public education programs can also be provided. Call weekdays between 9 A.M. and 5 P.M., EST.

Muscular Dystrophy Association
810 7th Avenue
New York, NY 10010
212-586-0808

o Occupational Safety

If you have a complaint about a work-related accident or are concerned about dangerous working conditions, call the Occupational Safety and Health Administration (OSHA). Staff members will answer your inquiries and investigate your complaint. Check the local telephone directory to see if there's a regional office near you; it will be listed under the U.S. Labor Department. If you are unable to locate the number, call the Washington office listed below. It is open every weekday from 8:15 A.M. until 4:45 P.M., EST.

Most states have "COSHs"—Committees on Occupational Safety and Health—such as NYCOSH, the New York Committee on Occupational Safety and Health. COSHs are private nonprofit organizations usually formed by scientists, physicians, union activists, and members of the public interested in occupational health. Most will answer questions from the general public. The information on—and phone numbers of—your local COSH is available from OSHA.

U.S. Department of Labor
Occupational Safety and Health Administration
  (OSHA)
Room N3637
Washington, DC 20210
202-523-8151

○ Organ Donation

The Living Bank operates a registry and referral service for people who want to commit their tissues, bones, vital organs, or bodies to transplantation or research on death. For more information or emergency donations call anytime; the line is answered 24 hours a day, seven days a week.

The Living Bank
P.O. Box 6725
Houston, TX 77265
800-528-2971
713-528-2971 (In Texas)

○ Orphan Drugs and Rare Diseases

NICODARD, a component of the National Health Information Clearinghouse, gathers and disseminates information on orphan drugs and products (these include those drugs, devices, foods, and biological agents that are used to prevent rare diseases and are, as a result, not widely available owing to their limited commercial interest) and rare diseases (any disease or condition with fewer than 200,000 reported cases in the United States). Questions are answered by information specialists with access to NHIC's computer data base, library, and reference system. Staff can also direct you to a self-help group. The line is answered on weekdays from 9 A.M. to 5 P.M., EST.

National Information Center for Orphan Drugs
  and Rare Diseases (NICODARD)
Office of Disease Prevention and Health
  Promotion
National Health Information Clearinghouse
P.O. Box 1133
Washington, DC 20013–1133
800-336-4797
703-522-2590 (In Virginia and the Washington,
  DC, metropolitan area)

○ Ostomy

The United Ostomy Association, composed of people who have had an ostomy (an operation to create an artificial anus), provides aid and information to those who have had ostomy surgery, to medical professionals, and to the public. Referrals and support group information are available. You can call any day of the week between 8 A.M. and 5 P.M., PST.

United Ostomy Association
2001 W. Beverly Boulevard
Los Angeles, CA 90057
213-413-5510

O Parkinson's Disease

If you're wondering what Parkinson's is or what can be done about it, call the National Parkinson Foundation. Staff members will answer any question you have and provide written information upon request. Referrals to medical professionals are also available. A trained staff member will answer your call weekdays from 8 A.M. to 5 P.M., EST.

National Parkinson Foundation
1501 N.W. 9th Avenue
Miami, FL 33136
800-327-4545
800-433-7022 (In Florida, except Miami)
305-547-6666 (In Miami)

The Parkinson's Education Program will provide you with information about patient support groups and referrals to physicians. Upon request, they will send you a copy of their newsletter, a glossary of definitions, and a publications catalog. The telephone is answered on weekdays between 7 A.M. and 5 P.M., PST; after hours, leave a message on an answering machine.

Parkinson's Education Program
1800 Park Newport #302
Newport Beach, CA 92660
800-344-7872
714-640-0218 (In California)

O Pelvic Inflammatory Disease (PID) See Health: Women's Health Network; Pregnancy, Birthing, and Family Planning: General Information.

O Phobias

The Phobia Society is a national nonprofit organization of phobics psychiatrists, psychologists, and other interested people. It provides general information on phobias, anxiety disorders, and treatment alternatives. Referrals to trained professionals are also available. Over-the-phone counseling is not available. Call any time. An answering machine will record your call and someone will get back to you.

The Phobia Society
5820 Hubbard Drive
Rockville, MD 20852
301-231-9350

o **Physical Fitness Programs** See *Sports and Athletics: Physical Fitness Programs.*

o **Physical Handicaps** (See also *Business: Accommodating the Handicapped; Education: Resources for the Learning Disabled and Handicapped; Reading and Writing: Books for the Blind and Physically Handicapped.*)

The primary goal of the National Easter Seal Society is to help people who have disabilities reach their full potential. Contrary to common belief, the society is designed to help not just children but anyone who is disabled from any cause, be it disease, illness, injury, or accident. When you call, a staff member will provide you with information on rehabilitation services, including physical, occupational, and speech-language therapies; vocational evaluation and training; camping and recreation; and psychological counseling. There are 800 affiliates of the society operating approximately 2000 facilities and programs in the country. Check your local phone directory for the number of the chapter nearest you; if you are unable to locate it, dial the 800 number printed below between 9 A.M. and 5 P.M., CST, on weekdays and a staff member will supply it.

National Easter Seal Society
2023 W. Ogden Avenue
Chicago, IL 60612
800-221-6827

Accent on Information is a computerized information service that supplies information on various topics to the disabled or to those who work with the disabled. Call weekdays from 8 A.M. to 4:30 P.M., CST.

Accent on Information
P.O. Box 700
Bloomington, IL 61702
309-378-2961

If you'd like information on rehabilitation programs for the homebound, call the Information Center for Handicapped Individuals. A staff member will provide you with details and offer referrals to services for the developmentally disabled. Information for foster parents of developmentally disabled children is also available. Call weekdays between 8:30 A.M. and 5 P.M., EST.

Information Center for Handicapped
  Individuals
605 G Street NW
Suite 202
Washington, DC 20001
202-347-4986

O **Poisons** See *Poison Control Centers.*

O **Premenstrual Syndrome** (See also *Pregnancy, Birthing, and Family Planning: Family Planning.*)

PMS ACCESS, a division of Madison Pharmacy Associates, Inc., provides information on premenstrual syndrome as well as support and referrals to physicians and clinics treating PMS in your area. Support-group information is also available, as are publications, cassettes, and other educational materials. Call any weekday between 9 A.M. and 5:30 P.M., CST.

PMS ACCESS
P.O. Box 9326
Madison, WI 53715
800-222-4PMS
608-257-8682 (In Wisconsin)

o Psychological Problems

Banking on the telephone's reputation as a "user-friendly instrument," Dr. Sidney Lecker, an attending psychiatrist at New York's Mount Sinai Medical Center, and Howard I. Glazer, an assistant attending psychologist at the Payne Whitney Psychiatric Center of Cornell University, also in New York City, founded Shrink Link, a no-frills telephone counseling service. Says Kathryn Hahner, a psychologist, former radio call-in show host, and the project director, "It's not exactly a crisis line or psychotherapy, but an area in-between." Anyway, weekdays from 9 A.M. to 9 P.M., EST, you can call and get professional advice on solving your problems. The cost is $15 for 10 minutes payable by VISA, MasterCard, or American Express. Referrals to private doctors and psychiatric centers are also available.

Shrink Link
Stress Control
320 E. 65th Street
New York, NY 10021
800-336-NEED
212-288-0606 (In New York)

If you're not sure where to go for psychological counseling, psychotherapy, or psychoanalysis, call the National Institute of Mental Health. They'll direct you to a mental health center in your area. The telephone is answered every weekday from 8 A.M. to 4:30 P.M., EST.

National Institute of Mental Health
Public Inquiries Section
Parklawn Building
Room 15CO5
5600 Fishers Lane
Rockville, MD 20857
301-443-4513

o Radiation Victims

The nuclear policies of the United States have left a trail of radiation victims—uranium miners, nuclear workers, atomic veterans, and people living downwind of nuclear-weapons test sites and near nuclear facilities. If you feel your health has been endangered by working or living in or around a nuclear facility, call the number listed below. A staff member will put you in touch with an organization in your area that can help you in the areas of research, litigation, legislation, and public education. Educators and other professionals are also encouraged to call for information; publications are available for a small cost. The office is open every weekday from 9 A.M. to 5 P.M., EST.

National Committee for Radiation Victims
236 Massachusetts Avenue NE
Suite 506
Washington, DC 20002
202-543-1070

o Reproductive Health (See also *Pregnancy, Birthing, and Family Planning: Family Planning.*)

Choice is a consumer advocacy group that provides callers with general information about reproductive health care. The staff can also give you a list of questions to ask a physician who has advised surgery before you agree to the operation. Referrals are made only to health-care professionals within Philadelphia and the surrounding five-county area. Call any weekday between 8:30 A.M. and 5 P.M., EST.

Choice
Sheridan Building
125 S. 9th Street, 6th Floor
Philadelphia, PA 19107
215-567-2904

o Second Surgical Opinion

If you're not sure whether that knee operation your doctor recommended is imperative to your health and you'd like a second opinion, call the Second Surgical Opinion Hotline.

Not only will the staff discuss, generally, nonemergency surgery with you; they will also give you the name and address of a surgeon in your area who has agreed to be a second-opinion consultant for the program. The hotline can also provide you with the name of a surgeon in your area if you suspect surgery is necessary. Publications are available upon request. Call weekdays and Saturday between 8 A.M. and 8 P.M., EST.

Second Surgical Opinion Hotline
National Second Surgical Opinion Program
330 Independence Avenue SW
Washington, DC 20201
800-638-6833
800-492-6603 (In Maryland)

○ **Self-Help Groups** See *Self-Help Groups.*

○ **Sex Therapy**

AASECT, a nonprofit educational association, was founded in 1967 by professionals who recognized the need for the development of standards for sex education, counseling, and therapy. Its membership is multidisciplinary and includes physicians, psychologists, ministers, counselors, sociologists, family-planning specialists, nurses, social workers, educators, and marriage and family therapists. If you are looking for a sex education therapist or counselor but don't know where to turn, call AASECT; a staff member will refer you to an agency or professional in your area. The office is open every weekday from 9 A.M. to 4:45 P.M., EST.

American Association of Sex Educators,
    Counselors, and Therapists (AASECT)
11 Dupont Circle NW
Suite 220
Washington, DC 20036
202-462-1171

○ Sexually Transmitted Diseases (See also *Pregnancy, Birthing, and Family Planning: Family Planning.*)

If you're concerned that you might have a sexually transmitted disease, call the VD Hotline. The specially trained staff member will provide free (and confidential) answers to all your questions and will refer you to a clinic or a physician in your area. Publications are available upon request. Don't be discouraged if you receive a busy signal the first few times you call: the hotline receives between 300 and 400 calls a day, but you will get through. The line is open 24 hours a day, every day of the year.

VD Hotline
American Social Health Association
260 Sheridan
Suite 307
Palo Alto, CA 94306
800-227-8922
800-982-5883 (In California)

○ Sickle Cell Anemia

The staff at the Sickle Cell Anemia Foundation of Greater New York will provide you with information about the services available nationwide for sickle cell anemia sufferers and their families. They will also provide referrals to physicians and organizations working to overcome the disease. Counseling is not, in general, provided. The office is open weekdays from 10 A.M. to 5 P.M., EST.

Sickle Cell Anemia Foundation of Greater New
  York
209 W. 125th Street
Room 208
New York, NY 10027
212-865-1201

○ Skin See *Hair and Skin Care: Skin.*

O **Smoking** (See also *Civil Rights: Nonsmokers' Rights.*)

Smokenders will send you or your company free information on the oldest, largest, and most successful smoking cessation program in the United States (the organization boasts an 80 percent success rate). Smokenders doesn't require you to go cold turkey; nor do you even have to exert much will power. In fact, you go on smoking for the first four weeks. Call weekdays 9 A.M. to 5 P.M., CST.

Smokenders
P.O. Box 3146
Glen Ellyn, IL 60138
800-323-1126
312-790-3328 (In Illinois)

The Stop Smoking Hotline is a series of tape-recorded messages, suggestions, and support for the smoker and ex-smoker. The series begins on the first Monday of the month and continues throughout the month, but you needn't begin on that Monday to benefit: the tips and reinforcements work as autonomous daily reminders as well. Call any day of the week, 24 hours a day. (This program is sponsored by the American Cancer Society, the Francois L. and Meta C. Schwarz Special Medical Fund of Lenox Hill Hospital's Department of Medicine, and Lenox Hill Hospital's Health Education Center.)

Stop Smoking Hotline
Lenox Hill Hospital
100 E. 77th Street
New York, NY 10021
212-794-8700

The Fresh Start program, sponsored by the American Cancer Society, relies on behavior-modification techniques to encourage smokers to stop their habit. There are two basic programs. The first is made up of four sessions (usually an hour per session), and run by former smokers. It is offered to companies only. The second is a ten-part program which is offered to both individuals and firms. The fees, which are modest, vary across the country. For more information, call a local cancer society listed under "American Cancer Society" or "Cancer Society" in your phone book. If you can't find a listing, call the national headquarters in New York City at the number listed below. It is open weekdays from 9 A.M. to 5 P.M., EST.

American Cancer Society
777 Third Avenue
New York, NY 10022
212-599-8200

o Spina Bifida

The Spina Bifida information and referral center, a service of the Spina Bifida Association of America, provides general information on spina bifida to consumers and health professionals. If you wish, the center will supply you with the name and address of the spina bifida chapter nearest you. Your call will be answered on weekdays between 9 A.M. and 5 P.M., CST.

Spina Bifida Information and Referral
343 S. Dearborn
Chicago, IL 60604
800-621-3141
312-663-1562 (In Illinois)

o Spinal Cord Injury

The Spinal Cord Society's primary concern is raising funds for research on reversing paralysis caused by spinal cord injury, but the staff will provide you with general information and, upon request, send you a copy of their monthly newsletter. Call any weekday between 9 A.M. and 5 P.M., CST.

Spinal Cord Society
2410 Lakeview Drive
Fergus Falls, MN 56537
800-328-8253
800-862-0179 (In Minnesota)

○ Stress and Tension

Tied up in knots? Call Lenox Hill Hospital's Relaxation Line. This 5-minute prerecorded message offers instructions on how to relax without drugs as you listen. The tape is ready to help you overcome stress and tension 24 hours a day, year round.

Relaxation Line
Lenox Hill Hospital
Health Education Center
100 E. 77th Street
New York, NY 10021
212-517-9550

○ Stuttering

The National Center for Stuttering provides information to parents of young children who stutter and refers older children and adults who stutter to treatment workshops. Training-session information for therapists is also available. Call any weekday between 9 A.M. and 5 P.M., EST; after hours, you may leave a message on the answering machine and someone will return your call shortly.

National Center for Stuttering
200 E. 33d Street
New York, NY 10016
800-221-2483
212-532-1460 (In New York)

○ Sudden Infant Death Syndrome

The National SIDS Foundation will provide you with medical information about sudden infant death syndrome as well as referrals. Information about support groups in your area may also be obtained here. Your call will be picked up anytime between 8 A.M. and 5 P.M., EST, on weekdays. After that, an answering machine will record your message.

National SIDS Foundation
2 Metro Plaza
Suite 205
8240 Professional Place
Landover, MD 20785
800-221-SIDS
301-459-3388 or **-3389** (In Maryland)

The National Sudden Infant Death Syndrome Clearinghouse serves parents and professionals interested in sudden infant death syndrome. General information, as well as referrals to support groups and physicians, is available weekdays between 8:30 A.M. and 5 P.M., EST.

The National Sudden Infant Death Syndrome
  Clearinghouse
3520 Prospect Street NW
Ground Floor
Suite 1
Washington, DC 20057
202-625-8410

○ **Toxic Shock Syndrome** See *Health: Women's Health Network; Pregnancy, Birthing, and Family Planning: General Information.*

○ **Urinary Tract Infection**

The symptoms of a urinary tract infection (UTI) are known to most women: an urgent need to urinate, burning with urination, and, occasionally, blood in the urine. UTIs are not life-threatening conditions (although it may seem that way at the time), and most respond readily to brief antibiotic therapy. However, many women suffer UTIs repeatedly; traditional urologists, responding to the symptoms, prescribe more antibiotics (even when no infection is apparent in the urine). When the woman experiences no relief, the urologist recommends tranquilizers and psychotherapy. But Dr. Larrian Gillespie, founder of the Women's Clinic for Interstitial Cystitis, has recognized and begun treating interstitial cystitis, the inflammation of the bladder surface caused by the use of antibiotics in the absence of infection. If you'd like more information about the causes and prevention of UTIs, call Dr. Gillespie (ask her about the diaphragm and cystitis). Referrals to local physicians are available, as are the names of other women in your area who have suffered from interstitial cystitis and are willing to share their experiences. The office is open from noon to 5 P.M., PST, on Mondays, 9 A.M. to 6 P.M. on Tuesday, Wednesday, and Thursday, and from 9 A.M. to noon on Fridays.

Larrian Gillespie, M.D.
Women's Clinic for Interstitial Cystitis
11633 San Vincente Boulevard
Suite 306
Brentwood, CA 90049
213-820-4631

O **Vaginal Infections**   See *Health: Women's Health Network; Pregnancy, Birthing, and Family Planning: General Information.*

O Women's Health Network

The National Women's Health Network, a national public interest organization devoted exclusively to women's health, has, since 1976, worked to promote responsible humane health care for all women. As a clearinghouse, the network provides information on a broad range of issues pertaining to women's health, including vaginal infections, the Dalkon Shield, Depo-Provera, contraceptive sponges, the cervical cap, abortion, and maternal and child health care. As an advocate for women's health, the network will, when necessary, take legal action. Referrals to women's health centers across the country and copies of studies and articles covering relevant issues are available. Consumers and professionals are encouraged to call any weekday between 9 A.M. and 5 P.M., EST.

National Women's Health Network
224 7th Street SE
Washington, DC 20003
202-543-9222

o **Women's Sports Medicine** See *Sports and Athletics: Women's Sports Foundation.*

• HEALTH INFORMATION LIBRARY

Tel-Med is a free telephone health library for the public offering tapes on topics approved by Lenox Hill Hospital physicians. The tapes provide neither diagnosis nor individual medical attention, but each does offer 3 to 5 minutes of basic information that will help you recognize early signs of disease. When you call, ask the Tel-Med operator for the number of the tape; it will then be played for you over the phone. Tel-Med accepts calls on weekdays from 9:30 A.M. to 4:30 P.M., EST.

Tel-Med
Lenox Hill Hospital
Health Education Center
100 E. 77th Street
New York, NY 10021
212-794-2200

Topic	Tape Number

Alcoholism

Alcoholism: Scope of the Problem	942
So You Love an Alcoholic	945

Cancer—*Sponsored by the American Cancer Society, New York City Division*

Breast Cancer	6
Breast Self-Examination	3064
Cancer in Black Americans	3035
Cancer of the Bladder	521
Cancer of the Brain	522
Cancer of the Larynx	523
Cancer of the Prostate Gland	176
Cancer of the Skin	185
Cancer of the Stomach	525
Cancer, the Preventable or Curable Disease	181
Childhood Leukemia	3059
Colorectal Cancer	3079
Hodgkin's Disease	184
Laetrile	528
Leukemia	3060
Lung Cancer	179
Mammography	526
Oral Cancer	524
Radiation Therapy for Cancer	188
Rehabilitation of the Breast Cancer Patient	178
Seven Warning Signs of Cancer	183
Uterine Cancer	186
What is a PAP Test?	182

Seven Paths to Cancer Prevention—*Sponsored by the American Cancer Society, New York City Division*

Diet and Cancer	701
Smoking and Cancer	702
Alcohol and Cancer	703
Stress and Cancer	704

	Tape
Topic	*Number*

Drug Abuse—*Sponsored by the Auxiliary of Lenox Hill Hospital*

Eye, Ear, Nose, and Throat

Topic	Tape Number
Proper Eye Care	3004
Sinusitis	3056
Sore Throats	70
Thyroid Disease	3081
Tonsillectomy	18

Family Planning

Abortion	24
Artificial Insemination	69
Birth Control Pills	55
Diaphragm, Foam, and Condom	58
Explaining the IUD	56
Infertility	68
Natural Family Planning	3023
Pregnant?	12
The Rhythm Method	57
Tubal Ligation	53
Vasectomy: Birth Control for Men	1

First Aid

Animal Bites	118
Fainting	108
Poisoning by Mouth	96

Heart and Circulatory Disease

Anemia	34
Angina	30
Arteriosclerosis	29
Chest Pains	65
Cholesterol	600
Cigarette Smoking and Heart Disease	21
Congenital Heart Defects	3074
Congestive Heart Failure	3017
Diet and Heart Disease	23
Early Warning Signs of a Heart Attack	63

| | *Tape* |
| *Topic* | *Number* |

Public Information

"Love and Pain," a Talk by Archbishop Sheen	3003
Medical Insurance	430
Social Service Information	3070

Respiratory Disease and Allergies

Allergies	567
Bronchial Asthma	576
Chronic Bronchitis	3052
Chronic Cough	581
Flu	38
Hay Fever	90
Pulmonary Emphysema	13
Pneumonia	3067
Shortness of Breath	582

Skin

Acne	172
Allergies	567
Baldness and Falling Hair	193
Circumcision	3083
Dandruff	79
Eczema	3086
Edema	3075
Impetigo	83
Itching Skin	518
Old Age Freckles	86
Plastic Surgery	1040
Psoriasis	82
Ringworm	80
Shingles	124

Sleep Information

| Dreams | 3058 |
| How to Fall Asleep | 3015 |

• HOME MAINTENANCE

O Appliance Repair (See also *Automobiles: Repair.*)

If you're a do-it-yourselfer, a call to the GE Answer Center's toll-free number could save you a bundle. Say you want to service your refrigerator. A GE technician can search an extensive data base for the information on your particular model, obtain a breakdown of parts to determine which ones are needed, and lead you through the necessary repair steps.

The answer center handles queries regarding all GE products and services—everything from light bulbs to computer time sharing. You may order use-and-care literature or complain about a particular model at this number any hour of the day, any day of the week, holidays included.

GE Answer Center
9500 Williamsburg Park Plaza
Louisville, KY 40222
800-626-2000

Whirlpool was one of the first companies in the appliance industry to set up a national toll-free number for consumers, and Whirlpool's Cool-Line will answer queries on everything from cooking a turkey in a microwave oven to repairing a washing machine clogged with sand. With amusement (and some pride) the company collects anecdotes from consumer comments on applications of Whirlpool technology that exceed the designer's original conceptions and considers this information when developing new designs. Mechanically inclined consumers may arrange to purchase step-by-step repair manuals for under $8, and consumer educators may request materials on appliance design, safety, energy use, and performance. Use-and-care manuals are also available, as are suggestions for where to take your appliance for servicing. The Cool-Line is open around the clock, with technical consultants on call weekdays from 8 A.M. to 9:30 P.M., EST, and from 9:30 A.M. to 4:30 P.M. on Saturdays.

Cool-Line™
Whirlpool Corporation
Benton Harbor, MI 49022
800-253-1301
800-253-1121 (In Alaska and Hawaii)
800-632-2243 (In Michigan)

MACAP, a group of independent consumer experts, receives comments and complaints from appliance owners, studies industry practices, and advises industry of ways to improve its service to consumers. If you have a complaint about a major appliance (compactor, dishwasher, home laundry equipment, refrigerator, etc.) and have attempted, without success, to solve your problem by calling the dealer or repair service recommended by the dealer and then calling or writing the customer relations office at the manufacturer's main headquarters, call MACAP weekdays between 8:30 A.M. and 5 P.M., CST. MACAP will put you on track toward rectifying the situation.

Major Appliance Consumer Action Panel
  (MACAP)
20 N. Wacker Drive
Chicago, IL 60606
800-621-0477
312-984-5858 (In Illinois, Alaska, and Hawaii)

Accredited Technicians will put residents of Massachusetts, Rhode Island, and parts of Connecticut and New Hampshire in touch with a local authorized repairer for diagnosis and repair of an appliance on either a factory warranty or a COD basis. A variable fee for in-home diagnosis is quoted on arrangement of an appointment. Accredited Technicians handles only a limited number of brands, so be sure to ask whether your appliance is covered before incurring charges. Call weekdays between 8 A.M. and 6 P.M., EST, and Saturdays between 8 A.M. and 1 P.M.

Accredited Technicians
Building Five
480 Neponset Street
Canton, MA 02021
800-343-1321 (In Connecticut, New
  Hampshire, and Rhode Island)
800-532-9539 (In Massachusetts)

○ **Carpets and Rugs** (See also *Fabrics and Textiles: Stain Removal.*)

The Carpet and Rug Institute will answer any question you have about purchasing carpets and rugs. Upon request, Georgia residents will be mailed a price list to help them comparison shop and can be referred to local retailers. The institute's telephone is answered weekdays from 8:30 A.M. to noon and 1 P.M. to 5 P.M., EST.

Carpet and Rug Institute
P.O. Box 2048
Dalton, GA 30722
404-278-3176

○ **Energy Conservation**

After thirty years as a propane gas dealer, Norval Hepler turned his energies from selling a dwindling resource to encouraging wider use of a renewable one: the jojoba (he-'ho-be) plant. Hepler built a retirement hobby exploring the potential of this versatile plant into a distributorship of products for preventive maintenance of automotive equipment. His current customers are South Dakota farmers who service their tractors from front to back with jojoba-based products. And jojoba isn't the only natural resource the conservation-minded Hepler has faith in. He's also marketing a whirlpool-like device that uses an air pump rather than a water pump to provide agitation for a therapeutic massage. Hepler will be happy to share his philosophy of renewable resources for preventive maintenance if you call his office weekdays between 8 A.M. and 9 A.M., CST.

Jojoba Advisory Service
Friendly Gas, Inc.
Platte, SD 57369
800-843-3363
800-952-3002 (In South Dakota)

A call to the Conservation and Renewable Energy Inquiry and Referral Service, funded by the U.S. Department of Energy, could save research time by providing bibliographic information on what the agency calls "short-term" renewable energy. The service also provides consumers with general information about heating and cooling equipment for the home, insulation, fuel wood, and energy-efficient landscaping. For more specific advice or information, the staff will point you toward appropriate sources. The CAREIRS line is open weekdays from 9 A.M. to 5 P.M., EST.

Conservation and Renewable Energy
  Inquiry and Referral Service (CAREIRS)
P.O. Box 8900
Silver Spring, MD 20907
800-523-2929
800-233-3071 (In Alaska and Hawaii)
800-462-4983 (In Pennsylvania)

The Energy Conservation Center is staffed by specialists who can provide you with information to solve your specific energy needs. General information on conserving energy, including weatherization services, appliance efficiency, and rebates, will also be provided. Upon request, they'll send you publications on air conditioner and heat pump rebates, loans, and home energy audits. Call weekdays from 9 A.M. to 5 P.M., EST.

Energy Conservation Center
Public Service Electric & Gas Company
P.O. Box 1258
Newark, NJ 07101
800-854-4444

○ Lumber

Originally set up for dealers handling pressure-treated lumber impregnated with the chemical it manufactures, the hotline of the Osmose Wood Preserving Company has rapidly become a treasured resource for savvy do-it-yourselfers. The hotline is a direct connection to both technical and practical information. You can learn not only how treated lumber responds to moisture but also how it accepts stains or paints and much more. Osmose also offers building plans for backyard construction of picnic tables, gazebos, and children's play structures and will direct you to the nearest pressure-treated lumber dealer. The hotline is staffed weekdays between 9 A.M. and 5 P.M., EST.

Osmose Wood Preserving Hotline
Osmose Wood Preserving Company of
  America, Inc.
Drawer O
Griffen, GA 30224
800-522-WOOD

○ Mobile Homes See *Mobile Home Safety Standards.*

○ Plumbing

Genova Plumbers is a manufacturer of gutters and plastic fittings, and the company hotline will suggest products to help you redirect that water that's now coursing through your living room ceiling. The staff can also suggest solutions to more technical plumbing problems. The hotline operates weekdays from 8 A.M. to 5 P.M., EST.

Genova Plumbers Hotline
7034 East Court Street
Davison, MI 48423
800-521-7488
800-572-5398 (In Michigan)

○ Real Estate Appraisals

The International Association of Assessing Officers, an organization of trained property assessors, will provide you with information on how the assessed value of your property relates to market value and how frequently land parcels are visited. They will also answer your questions about the work sheets assessors use to determine property value and tax assessments. The association welcomes your questions weekdays between 8:30 A.M. and 4:30 P.M., CST.

International Association of Assessing Officers
1313 E. 60th Street
Chicago, IL 60637
312-947-2069

○ Soap and Detergent

The Soap and Detergent Association's Consumer Education Service Department will try to answer questions about any aspect of soaps and detergents. Most of their calls are from students, homemakers, advertising agencies, and others interested in enzymes, housecleaning, and laundry products. The staff is quite friendly and will tell you all about their free publications when you call. Give them a try on weekdays between 9 A.M. and 4:45 P.M., EST.

Soap and Detergent Association
475 Park Avenue South
New York, NY 10016
212-725-1262

○ Swimming Pools See *Sports and Athletics: Swimming.*

○ Woodworking

You're in the middle of a woodworking project and can't put the pieces together. A call to this maker of bandsaws, jigsaws, joiners, and other woodworking tools might yield a solution. If an answer to your dilemma is not immediately forthcoming, the Shopsmith staff will research your problem and call you back. Call weekdays between 9 A.M. and 6 P.M., EST, and Saturdays between 9 A.M. and 1 P.M.

Shopsmith, Inc.
6640 Poe Avenue
Dayton, OH 45414
800-543-7586

I

• INFORMATION CENTERS

○ General

Every county in the United States has a cooperative extension office—that is, an office cooperating with a prominent university to extend expert information of special interest to the people of the locale. In rural areas, the extension office is usually the first place people call when they have a problem; in urban centers, these offices are less well known and certainly worth looking into; you'll find information or referrals on horticulture, nutrition, tenant affairs, and the care and handling of fabrics, to name just a few. Cooperative extension offices are listed in the local telephone book under the name of your county. In New York City, see the listings under Cornell University.

What time does the moon rise in Paris tonight? This is just one of the millions of questions asked of the Federal Information Center, a government-sponsored answer center which is willing to try to answer any question you have on any subject you're interested in. Although they can't guarantee that they'll have every bit of information that you need at hand, if they don't, they'll tell you who does. They can also provide you with more banal information such as the names, addresses, and telephone numbers of government agencies and programs. Call any weekday between 8 A.M. and 5 P.M., EST. The center puts out a brochure listing all the FICs across the nation and you can write to them and request a copy.

Federal Information Center
26 Federal Plaza
New York, NY 10278
212-264-4464

○ Lesbians and Gays

Want to know where the gay bars are in Washington, DC? Call the Gay Information and Assistance Service. This national clearinghouse of information on homosexual rights offers a wide range of information available to callers, including both legal counsel and referrals. Security-clearance information is also available. Because the service is staffed by volunteers, the phone is answered erratically, but an answering machine, when it works, will record your message and someone will get back to you shortly. The staff emphasizes that they are not a walk-in clinic. By the way, the service uses "homosexual" to describe both gays and lesbians.

Gay Information and Assistance Service
5020 Cathedral Avenue NW
Washington, DC 20016
202-363-3881

The staff at the National Gay Task Force will provide information about health-related matters, including AIDS. They also offer counseling to gay and lesbian youth. Referrals to victim-service agencies are also available. Call any weekday between 3 P.M. and 9 P.M., EST.

National Gay Task Force
80 Fifth Avenue
New York, NY 10011
800-221-7044
212-807-6016 (In New York, Alaska, and
    Hawaii)

○ Libraries

Despite our technocracy, libraries remain one of the most reliable, friendliest, and certainly most underrated sources of expert information around. We have listed seven major public libraries and indicated some of their special holdings.

Try your local library first; if someone there can't help you, call one of the libraries listed below. One is sure to provide you with the information you need.

Library of Congress
First and Independence Avenues
Washington, DC 20540
(8:30 A.M. to 9:30 P.M., EST, Monday–Friday;
    8:30 A.M. to 5 P.M. Saturday; 1 P.M. to 5 P.M.,
    Sunday) **202-287-5000**
Social and political science, American history, aeronautical literature, Chinese and Russian collections (the largest outside of Asia and the U.S.S.R.), papers of the presidents, a music collection containing 3 million items

Boston Public Library
666 Boylston Street
Boston, MA 02117
(9 A.M. to 9 P.M., EST, Monday–Thursday; 9
    A.M. to 5 P.M., Friday and Saturday)
    617-536-5400
Bowditch Library of mathematics and astronomy, Ticknor Library of Spanish and Portuguese books, Hunt Library of West Indian material, Galatea Collection of works on the history of women, Trent Collection of Defoe and Defoeana

Detroit Public Library
5201 Woodward Avenue
Detroit, MI 48202
(9:30 A.M. to 5 P.M., CST, Monday, Tuesday,
    Thursday, Friday; 9 A.M. to 5 P.M.,
    Wednesday; 9:30 A.M. to 5:30 P.M., Saturday)
    313-833-1000
History of Detroit, the old northwest territory, and adjacent Canadian areas; National Automotive History Collection; E. Azalia Hackley Memorial Collection on Afro-Americans in Music and the Performing Arts

Chicago Public Library
425 N. Michigan Avenue
Chicago, IL 60602
(9 A.M. to 7 P.M., CST, Monday–Thursday; 9
   A.M. to 6 P.M., Friday; 9 A.M. to 5 P.M.,
   Saturday) **312-269-2900**
Vivian G. Harsh Collection of Afro-American History and Literature; the James Ellsworth Papers relating to the Columbian Exposition; Goodman Theatre Collection of programs, photographs, and scrapbooks; and GAR Museum of Civil War relics

The New York Public Library
42d Street and Fifth Avenue
New York, NY 10036
The New York Public Library is peerless in its range of public-division information experts specializing in various subjects. If a question is too specialized or technical to be answered by the general telephone reference librarian, he or she will direct you to the appropriate division. (Because the general telephone reference operators receive over 1000 calls a day, they request your patience when calling.) Or you can dial direct; the numbers and hours are listed below. All divisions are located at the 42d Street branch unless otherwise noted.

General Reference Division
(9 A.M. to 6 P.M., EST,
   Monday–Friday; 10 A.M. to
   6 P.M., Saturday)
   212-340-0849

Slavonic Division
(10 A.M. to 6 P.M., EST,
   Monday, Wednesday,
   Friday, Saturday; 10 A.M.
   to 9 P.M., Tuesday)
   212-930-0714

*U.S. and Local History and
   Genealogy*
(10 A.M. to 9 P.M., EST,
   Monday–Wednesday; 10
   A.M. to 6 P.M., Thursday–
   Saturday) **212-930-0828**

*Rare Book Room and
   Manuscripts*
(10 A.M. to 6 P.M., EST,
   Monday–Wednesday,
   Friday–Saturday)
   212-930-0819

Maps
(10 A.M. to 6 P.M., EST,
   Monday, Wednesday,
   Friday; 10 A.M. to 9 P.M.,
   Tuesday) **212-930-0587**

Jewish Division
(10 A.M. to 6 P.M., EST,
   Monday, Wednesday,
   Friday; 10 A.M. to 6 P.M.,
   Tuesday; 1 P.M. to 6 P.M.,
   Saturday) **212-930-0601**

Science and Technology
(10 A.M. to 6 P.M., EST,
   Monday, Wednesday–
   Saturday; 10 A.M. to 9 P.M.,
   Tuesday) **212-930-0574**

Economics
(10 A.M. to 6 P.M., EST,
   Monday, Wednesday–
   Saturday; 10 A.M. to 9 P.M.,
   EST, Tuesday)
   212-930-0724

Oriental Division
(10 A.M.–6 P.M., EST,
   Monday, Wednesday,
   Friday, Saturday; 10 A.M.
   to 9 P.M., Tuesday)
   212-930-0716

Black Culture
Schomburg Center for
   Research and Black
   Culture
1515 Lenox Avenue
New York, NY 10037
(12 P.M. to 8 P.M., EST,
   Monday–Wednesday; 10
   A.M. to 6 P.M., Thursday–
   Saturday) **212-862-4000**

Patents Division
521 W. 43d Street
New York, NY 10036
(9 A.M. to 5 P.M., EST,
   Monday–Saturday)
   212-714-8529

Newspaper Annex
521 W. 43d Street
New York, NY 10036
(9 A.M. to 5 P.M., EST,
   Monday–Saturday)
   212-714-8520

National Agricultural Library
U.S. Department of Agriculture
10301 Baltimore Boulevard
Beltsville, MD 20705
(8 A.M. to 4:30 P.M., EST, weekdays)
   301-344-3755
Nine thousand books of records of purebred registration of
domestic animals; one of the most renowned collections of

blooded stock, herd, flock, and stud books in world; Horticultural Trade Catalogues Collection, largest apicultural collection in the United States, collection of original works of Linnaeus

National Library of Medicine
8600 Rockville Pike
Bethesda, MD 20209
(8:30 A.M. to 5 P.M., EST, Monday–Saturday)
   301-496-6095
This is the world's largest research library in a single scientific and professional field; the collection count stands today at 3.25 million items, including the first edition of Robert Burton's *The Anatomy of Melancholy* and the first English translation of Fracastoros's *Syphilis*.

o Product Information

The Consumer Products Safety Commission is a federal agency charged with reducing injuries associated with consumer products found in and around the home; it is a useful source of information on many major purchases. Say you're buying a playpen and are concerned about toxicity, sturdiness, or the possibility of a toddler's head becoming wedged between the slats. The Consumer Products Safety Commission can scan its data bank for product recalls and pass on any warnings. The agency will also take complaints regarding product safety. Literature on specific products is also available. Call weekdays from 8:30 A.M. to 5 P.M., EST.

Consumer Products Safety Commission
1111 18th Street NW
Washington, DC 20207
800-638-CPSC

Consumers Union is one of the oldest and most reliable sources of consumer product testing and analysis. If you'd like to know whether a specific product has been tested, call the Information Services Department. If it has, you'll be directed to the issue of *Consumer Reports* in which the results are printed. (No test results are given over the telephone.) Call weekdays between 9 A.M. and 5 P.M., EST.

Information Services Department
Consumers Union of the United States, Inc.
256 Washington Street
Mt. Vernon, NY 10553
914-667-9400

○ Referrals

The National Referral Center in the Library of Congress is a free referral service which directs those who have questions concerning any subject to organizations, institutions, groups, or individuals who have specialized information and a willingness to share it. The referral service uses a subject-indexed, computerized file of 14,000 information resources; a description of each resource includes its special fields of interest and what types of information service it provides. The referral center is not able to furnish answers to specific questions or to provide bibliographic assistance. Inquiries are accepted weekdays between 8:30 A.M. and 5 P.M., EST.

Library of Congress
National Referral Center
Washington, DC 20540
202-287-5670

○ Women

Founded in 1971, the Women's Action Alliance develops educational programs and services that assist women and women's organizations. The alliance also provides interested persons with information about women's issues and programs, women's organizations, multiservice centers for women, program planning, organizational development, and fund-raising. Publications are available on economic development, nonsexist education and child rearing, and state-by-state directories of services and occupations. If the alliance can't help you, a staff member will refer you to someone who can. Call any weekday between the hours of 9 A.M. and 5 P.M., EST.

Women's Action Alliance, Inc.
370 Lexington Avenue
New York, NY 10017
212-532-8330

The staff of the Women's Help Hotline, established by the New York chapter of the National Organization for Women (NOW), will direct women living in the New York metropolitan area to sources of information about and aid in dealing with any problem engendered by sexism in our society. Most frequently, callers are directed to services that deal with discreet areas such as job discrimination, abortion, contraception, counseling, and child care. Check your local chapter of NOW to see if it provides a similar service. If not, contact the New York chapter; someone there may be able to put you in touch with an organization in your area that can help. The phone is answered on weekdays from 9:30 A.M. to 5 P.M., EST.

Women's Help Hotline
National Organization for Women (NOW)
15 W. 18th Street
New York, NY 10011
212-989-7230

o Women's History

About 120 years after the first Women's Rights Convention in Seneca Falls, New York, the National Women's Hall of Fame was founded ". . . to honor in perpetuity those women . . . whose contributions to the arts, athletics, business, education, government, the humanities, philanthropy and science, have been the greatest value for the development of their country." If you would like general information about any of their honorees (including Jane Addams, Susan B. Anthony,

Clara Barton, Elizabeth Blackwell, Pearl S. Buck, Rachel Carson, Mary Cassatt, Carrie Chapman Catt, Emily Dickinson, Amelia Earhart, Alice Hamilton, Helen Keller, Belva Lockwood, Margaret Mead, Lucretia Mott, Frances Perkins, Margaret Sanger, Bessie Smith, Elizabeth Cady Stanton, Sojourner Truth, Harriet Tubman, and fourteen others), call any weekday between 10 A.M. and 4 P.M., EST. The staff can also provide you with information about the evolution of the Hall of Fame and about efforts to preserve the Stanton House, the Bloomer House, and other historical sites in Seneca Falls.

The National Women's Hall of Fame
P.O. Box 335
Seneca Falls, NY 13148
315-568-8060

● INSURANCE

○ Commercial See *Business: Insurance.*

○ Personal See *Personal Finances: Insurance.*

J

• JOB COUNSELING

○ Disabled People See *Business: Accommodating the Handicapped.*

○ Displaced Homemakers (See also *Business: Developing Career and Family Options; Business: Services for Women.*)

The Displaced Homemakers Network is a national nonprofit organization of displaced homemakers, service providers, and other supporters that links individuals with counseling workshops and skills-training and job-placement programs. When you call, a staff member will provide the name and address of an agency near you that can help and, if you wish, will provide you with general information on displaced homemakers and the programs that serve them. Technical assistance is also provided to employers looking to develop programs that work for displaced homemakers. The office is open every weekday from 8 A.M. to 5 P.M., EST.

Displaced Homemakers Network
1010 Vermont Avenue NW
Suite 817
Washington, DC 20005
202-628-6767

○ Nontraditional Occupations See *Information Centers: Women.*

○ Occupational Safety See *Health: Occupational Safety.*

○ Older People See *Older People: Employment.*

L

• LAW

○ **Child Law** See *Children and Child Care: Child Law.*

○ **Consultation**

If you need help choosing a lawyer or would like to complain about an incompetent one, call the National Resource Center for Consumers of Legal Services. A staff member will help you evaluate your needs as a client and take action concerning your grievance. Information about setting up a legal services plan may also be obtained here. The office is open every weekday from 9 A.M. to 5 P.M., EST.

National Resource Center for Consumers of
  Legal Services
3254 Jones Court NW
Washington, DC 20007
202-338-0714

○ **Consumer Complaints** See *Consumer Complaint Services.*

○ **Disabled People's Rights** See *Business: Accommodating the Handicapped.*

○ **Discrimination**

The staff at the NAACP Legal Defense Fund will put you in touch with an attorney who can help if you find yourself in a situation where you feel you have been discriminated against because of your race or class. The office is open week-days from 9:30 A.M. to 5:30 P.M., EST.

NAACP Legal Defense and Educational Fund
99 Hudson Street, 16th Floor
New York, NY 10013
212-219-1900

○ **Families** See *Pregnancy, Birthing, and Family Planning: Family Planning.*

○ **Lesbians and Gays** (See also *Information Centers: Lesbians and Gays; Pregnancy, Birthing, and Family Planning: Lesbian Mothers.*)

Perhaps the most important function of Gay and Lesbian Advocates and Defenders (GLAD) is to give legal direction to lesbians and gays who are not sure whether legal involvement is necessary. In addition to helping you sort out your dilemma, a counselor will offer information about litigation and education work going on in the area of homosexual civil rights and will refer you to an attorney in your area if necessary. The staff of cooperating attorneys donate their time; GLAD does not charge clients legal fees. Hours are generally week-days from 9 A.M. to 5 P.M., EST. An answering machine will record your message if no one is in.

Gay and Lesbian Advocates and Defenders
   (GLAD)
P.O. Box 218
Boston, MA 02112
617-426-1350

○ **Radiation Victims** See *Health: Radiation Victims.*

○ Referrals

If you need help finding or choosing a lawyer, call the American Bar Association. A staff member will direct you to your local legal referral service, who will in turn advise you of your options. The ABA answers calls weekdays from 9 A.M. to 5 P.M., CST.

American Bar Association
Lawyer Referral and Information Service
1155 E. 60th Street
Chicago, IL 60637
312-332-1111

The National Legal Aid and Defender Association acts as a clearinghouse of organizations providing legal aid and defender services to those without the means to pay. For more information, call them any weekday between 9 A.M. and 5:30 P.M., EST.

National Legal Aid and Defender Association
1625 K Street NW
Washington, DC 20084
202-452-0620

○ Social Security Claims See *Older People: Social Security.*

○ Women (See also *Health: Women's Health Network.*)

The Women's Legal Defense Fund, a national membership organization dedicated to securing women's rights through advocacy and litigation, provides legal counseling to women on any legal matter engendered by sexism in our society (including pregnancy discrimination and economic inequity). One of their most important functions is to help women who are interested in retaining or changing their surnames. Because all state procedures differ (every woman is, however, legally permitted to use whatever name she chooses), the Legal Defense Fund serves primarily residents of Maryland, Virginia, and the District of Columbia. If you live outside this area, check your telephone directory for a local feminist organization or try the Women's Rights program at a nearby law school. If neither can help, call the Women's Legal Defense Fund; a staff member will direct you to a source of information. Referrals to local attorneys are also available. The office is open weekdays from 9 A.M. to 5 P.M., EST.

Women's Legal Defense Fund
2000 P Street NW
Washington, DC 20036
202-887-0364

○ Youth Law

The National Center for Youth Law's number is for use by both attorneys and children: attorneys can have finer points of the law cleared up, and children can find out how much they stand to lose or gain. Attorneys are standing by to help both every weekday between the hours of 9 A.M. and 5 P.M., PST.

National Center for Youth Law
1663 Mission Street, 5th Floor
San Francisco, CA 94103
415-543-3307

● LESBIANS AND GAYS

○ AIDS See *Health: AIDS.*

○ Civil Rights See *Law: Lesbians and Gays.*

○ Information Centers See *Information Centers: Lesbians and Gays.*

○ Parenting See *Pregnancy, Birthing, and Family Planning: Lesbian Mothers.*

M

- **MISSING CHILDREN** See *Children and Child Care: Missing and Exploited Children; Children and Child Care: Runaways.*

- **MOBILE HOME SAFETY STANDARDS**

The Manufactured Housing Institute, an organization of manufacturers and suppliers of factory-built homes, will supply consumers with information about manufactured-home safety and construction standards, zoning, and land development. Telephone inquiries are accepted weekdays between 8:30 A.M. and 5:30 P.M., EST.

Manufactured Housing Institute
1745 Jefferson Davis Highway
Suite 511
Arlington, VA 22202
703-979-6620

N

• NAME CHANGING AND RETENTION
See *Law: Women.*

• NEW YORK CITY

○ Consumer Services

Cityphone, a friendly and much-used information hotline covering places, services, and merchandise offerings in New York City, will help you locate whatever you need in the Big Apple, be it an exotic restaurant, a retinning service for copperware, or a rare breed of dog. The telephone is answered every weekday between 9 A.M. and 5 P.M., EST.

Cityphone
91 Fifth Avenue
New York, NY 10003
212-675-0900

○ History

The New York City Municipal Reference and Research Center has two divisions; between them they contain rooms of documents—both official and unofficial—pertaining to the city and its public history. The reference librarians are most willing to answer any question pertaining to the city's development, codes and regulations, fiscal crises, or anything else of interest to you. Each division is listed below with its special holdings.

Municipal Reference Library
Department of Records and Information
31 Chambers Street, Room 112
New York, NY 10007
(9 A.M. to 5 P.M., EST, weekdays) **212-566-4284**
Current information about New York City and general urban
issues, biographies of city and state officials, New York state
codes and regulations, clipping file for city fiscal crisis of 1975

Municipal Archives
31 Chambers Street, Room 101
New York, NY 10007
(9 A.M. to 4:30 P.M., EST, weekdays)
  212-566-5292
All but current information is held here, including nineteenth-
century-building docket books, histories of street names, and
histories of the city and the state

● **NUTRITION** See *Diet and Nutrition.*

○ **Children** See *Children and Child Care: Nutrition.*

O

• OCCUPATIONAL COUNSELING See *Job Counseling.*

• OLDER PEOPLE

○ Alzheimer's Disease See *Health: Alzheimer's Disease.*

○ Education

Want to learn how to use a computer? Study U.S. women writers? The ecology of Maine? Beekeeping? How about tai chi? Or astrophotography? If so, and if you're over 60 (the only requirement for admission), check out Elderhostel, an educational program that offers noncredit courses on a variety of liberal arts and sciences subjects at over 800 colleges, universities, and other educational institutions in the United States, Canada, Europe, Australia, and Asia. While participating, you will stay in a dormitory, eat at the campus dining facility, and have access to the educational, cultural, and recreational facilities at the host institution; your daily life will be shared with twenty to forty Elderhostel classmates. The cost is modest: $195 for a one-week program ($200 in Canada)—and that covers everything. Some scholarships for those who require financial assistance are available. For more information, call the number listed below any weekday between 9 A.M. and 5 P.M., EST.

Elderhostel
80 Boylston Street, Suite 400
Boston, MA 02116
617-426-7788

○ Employment

The National Council on the Aging is dedicated to helping forge a more equitable, caring, and enlightened society that will protect the rights of older Americans and expand their opportunities. The council has originated the Senior Community Service Employment Program, an agency designed to help older people secure employment and income. Information on training programs is available here, as is advice on where to go to find out about community service employment programs in your area. The office is open every weekday between 9 A.M. and 5 P.M., EST.

Senior Community Service Project
National Council on the Aging
600 Maryland Avenue SW
Washington, DC 20024
202-479-1200

○ Nursing Homes

The National Council of Senior Citizens is a volunteer organization that provides callers with information about nursing-home standards and regulations. If you'd like some help figuring out how to choose a nursing home, the council will give you a list of services to look for. If you'd like information on patients' rights, the council has that too. If, by chance, the staff can't answer your question, they'll refer you to someone who can. Call any weekday between 10 A.M. and 3 P.M., EST. You may leave a message on their answering machine between 9 A.M. and 10 A.M. and between 3 P.M. and 5 P.M. Someone will get back to you shortly.

National Council of Senior Citizens
925 15th Street NW
Washington, DC 20005
202-347-8800

○ Retirement

The American Association of Retired Persons (AARP) is an organization of retired persons over 50; AARP will give you information on a variety of nationwide services and resources available to retired people over 50. The staff answers calls weekdays between 9 A.M. and 5 P.M., EST.

American Association of Retired Persons
 (AARP)
1909 K Street NW
Washington, DC 20049
202-872-4700

o Services

If you need legal assistance or just want information on services that cater to the elderly, call your local chapter of the National Council on the Aging. A staff member will provide you with information on programs specially designed to help the elderly and will refer you to sources of more explicit help or information. If you can't find a chapter near you, call the Washington office listed below. Phone inquiries are taken weekdays between 9 A.M. and 5 P.M., EST.

National Council on the Aging
600 Maryland Avenue SW
West Wing 100
Washington, DC 20024
800-424-9046

Printed in large type, *Silver Pages* is a telephone directory designed for use by senior citizens. The directory is divided into three sections: There is a listing of local businesses offering discounts to people over 60; a listing of national advertisers such as restaurant chains that offer special discounts to senior citizens; and an information and referral section featuring free or nonprofit legal, medical, nutritional, and transportation services. For more information on where and how you can obtain a copy or if you would like to lodge a complaint against an advertiser, dial the number listed below. Someone will be happy to help you every weekday between 7:45 A.M. and 4:15 P.M., CST.

Silver Pages
1830 Craig Park Court
St. Louis, MO 63146
800-252-6060

o Social Security

If you have a question about your Social Security benefits or Medicare, call your local Social Security office; the number should be listed in your local telephone directory. If you can't find the number, call the national headquarters listed below or consult your post office for the schedule of visits of Social Security representatives. The national office is open weekdays between 8:30 A.M. and 5 P.M., EST.

Social Security Administration
Office of Public Inquiries
6401 Security Boulevard
Baltimore, MD 21235
301-594-7705

The staff at the National Organization of Social Security Claimants Representatives will provide callers with the names and addresses of attorneys within the caller's area who specialize in claims against the Social Security Administration. Most member attorneys work on a contingency basis. The office is open every weekday from 9 A.M. to 6 P.M., EST.

National Organization of Social Security
  Claimants Representatives
19 E. Central Avenue
Pearl River, NY 10965
800-431-2804
914-735-8812 (In New York; call collect)

○ **Volunteering** See *Volunteering.*

○ Women

The Older Women's League (OWL), a national grassroots organization, is dedicated to providing support for its members, achieving economic and social equity for its constituents, and improving the image and status of older women. Their present concerns include Social Security (protecting present benefits and pressing for a correction of present inequities), pension rights (working to correct the inequities in public and private systems), health insurance (lobbying for access to affordable health insurance), caretaker support services (working to promote services that offer relief to homebound caretakers), jobs (combating age and sex discrimination), and budget cuts (working to redirect national budget priorities). If you have any questions about the above areas or would like the address of your local chapter, call OWL weekdays between 9 A.M. and 5 P.M., EST. The staff stresses two things: first, OWL supports both midlife and older women; second, no over-the-phone counseling is offered.

Older Women's League (OWL)
1325 G Street NW
Washington, DC 20005
202-783-6686

• OUTDOORS AND RECREATION (See also *Sports and Athletics.*)

○ General Information

If you have a question about any aspect of natural history, geography, or the allied sciences, call the National Geographic Society Library. The collection is enormous (the library contains, among other things, the entire contents of General A.

W. Greely's polar library), and the staff is amiable. The reference librarian will answer your question any weekday from 8:30 A.M. to 5 P.M., EST.

National Geographic Society Library
16th and M Streets NW
Washington, DC 20036
202-857-7787

o Boating Classes

If you're interested in taking a free boating-safety class, call the U.S. Foundation for Boating Safety. The foundation will provide you with a list of classes offered in your area sponsored by either the Red Cross, the U.S. Coast Guard Auxiliary, or the U.S. Power Squadron, and the only cost for you is the price of the materials. A staff member will be happy to help you any weekday between 9 A.M. and 5:30 P.M., EST.

U.S. Foundation for Boating Safety
880 S. Pickett Street
Alexandria, VA 22304
800-336-BOAT
703-823-9550 (In Virginia)

o Boating Safety

The Boating Safety Hotline was established in June 1985 and patterned after the popular Auto Safety Hotline to provide safety information on any recreational craft regulated as a boat—from the tiniest dinghy to a 65-foot Hatteras yacht. Available recall information coincides with the five-year federal statute of limitations on a manufacturer's obligation to correct a defect. Although the staff is not prepared to answer nonsafety questions, they may be able to put you on the right track to an answer. The staff also takes complaints and reports on possible safety defects, assists consumers who are having difficulty getting action on recalls, and provides literature on federal requirements for recreational boats. The line operates weekdays from 8 A.M. to 4 P.M., EST.

Boating Safety Hotline
Office of Boating, Public, and Consumer Affairs
U.S. Coast Guard Headquarters
Washington, DC 20593
800-368-5647
202-472-2385 (In Washington, DC, and Alaska)

o Conservation

The Natural Resources Library is a federally funded library that will answer any question you have about conservation, energy and power, land use, parks, fish, wildlife, and mining. The library also contains some holdings on American Indians. Call any weekday between 8 A.M. and 5 P.M., EST.

U.S. Department of the Interior
Natural Resources Library
18th and C Streets NW
Washington, DC 20240
202-343-5815

If you have a question about wildlife, natural resources, conservation, ecology, or the environment, the National Wildlife Federation Library is the source to turn to. The library is open weekdays from 8 A.M. to 4:30 P.M., EST.

National Wildlife Federation Library
8925 Leesburg Pike
Vienna, VA 22180
703-790-4446

o Mountaineering

If you're interested in mountains or want some information about mountaineering, call the librarian at the Appalachian

Mountain Club. The librarian will answer any question you have about the history and the exploration of mountain areas. The library contains journals of mountain clubs from around the world and is open between noon and 4 P.M., EST, Wednesdays and Fridays.

Appalachian Mountain Club Library
5 Joy Street
Boston, MA 02108
617-523-0636

○ Ornithology

If you want to know the name of that pretty yellow bird that's nested in the rafters of your garage, call the National Audubon Society. The staff of the Information Services Department will provide you with answers to any question you have about ornithology and bird clubs and can supply you with general information about conservation of natural resources and natural history. The staff is not permitted to conduct in-depth research. The library is open every weekday from 9 A.M. to 5 P.M., EST.

Information Services Department
National Audubon Society Library
950 Third Avenue
New York, NY 10022
212-832-3200

P

● **PARENTING**   See *Pregnancy, Birthing, and Family Planning.*

○ **Adoption**   See *Children and Child Care: Adopting Special Children.*

○ **Lesbians**   See *Pregnancy, Birthing, and Family Planning: Lesbian Mothers.*

○ **Single**   See *Children and Child Care: Single Parents.*

● **PERFORMING ARTS**

○ **General Information**

The Performing Arts Library offers information and reference assistance on dance, theater, music, film, broadcasting, and all related areas of the performing arts. The library, which is a joint project of the Library of Congress and the Kennedy Center, encourages calls from both the public and professional artists. In addition, the library provides a national focus, through its computer terminal and audio links to the Library of Congress, for identifying the creative resources and materials necessary to the development of new works and productions in the performing arts. Feel free to call between 11 A.M. and 8:30 P.M., EST, Tuesday through Friday, and between 10 A.M. and 6 P.M. on Saturday.

Performing Arts Library
Roof Terrace Level
John F. Kennedy Center for the Performing
   Arts
Washington, DC 20566
202-287-6245 or **202-254-9803**

○ Theater

Beverly Kowalski-Firestone, one of a select group of English-speaking theater artists sent to Poland in 1977 to study and work within the acclaimed Polish Laboratory Theatre of Jerzy Grotowski, is presently completing a book entitled *The Cold Light of the Polish Laboratory Theatre* in which she details her reactions to the theories, experiments, and exercises at the lab. Dr. Firestone disagrees with those visionaries described by André Gregory in *My Dinner with André;* rather than considering Grotowski a liberating visionary, Dr. Firestone believes that he more clearly patterns the shamans of ancient exorcism rites. In addition to a history of the Teatr Laboratorium, Firestone has integrated sources from psychology, parapsychology, philosophy, religion, theater, mythology, and administration to support her perceptions of the essence and impact of this nontheater theater. Firestone, who also conducts workshops and presentations, will share her philosophy or answer any questions you have every weekday between 9 A.M. and 5 P.M., CST.

Beverly Kowalski-Firestone
500 N. Michigan Avenue
Suite 1400
Chicago, IL 60611
312-661-1700

● PERSONAL FINANCES

○ Banking   (See also *Business: Banking.*)

If you're concerned about the possibility that your bank may fail, a call to the Federal Deposit Insurance Corporation (FDIC) may ease your fear by describing the protections available under the consumer banking laws—provided that your bank has coverage. Complaints cannot be taken or resolved over the phone, but the FDIC will tell you how to route your complaint for proper handling and give you the address of your regional office. Information may be obtained weekdays from 9 A.M. to 5 P.M., EST.

Federal Deposit Insurance Corporation (FDIC)
550 17th Street NW
Washington, DC 20429
800-424-5488

○ Charities

The Philanthropic Advisory Service provides people interested in giving with data on 7000 national, nonprofit organizations and how they spend their money. For $1 the service will send you the publication *Give But Give Wisely*, a bimonthly list of the 400 organizations about which the most inquiries have been received from the public, the media, the government, and other better business bureaus (BBBs). The list contains the names of those that meet and don't meet the BBB's standards. The telephone is answered weekdays from 9 A.M. to 5 P.M., EST.

Philanthropic Advisory Service
Council of Better Business Bureaus, Inc.
1515 Wilson Boulevard
Arlington, VA 22209
703-276-0133

The National Charities Information Bureau will supply interested parties with reports on charitable organizations, detailing how much each organization has spent on activities and how much on administration. Upon request, they'll send you a copy of their "Wise Giving Guide," a brochure that lists 400 national nonprofit organizations. Call weekdays between 9 A.M. and 5 P.M., EST.

National Charities Information Bureau
19 Union Square West
New York, NY 10003
212-929-6300

○ Collectibles See *Collectibles.*

○ Commodities

If you're thinking of hiring a commodities broker but wonder if she or he has been involved in any shady dealings, call the Commodity Futures Trading Commission. The answering member will tell you if the broker or firm you're interested in has, to the commission's knowledge, been party to any fraudulent practices or unauthorized trade. The commission will also accept complaints. A member will answer your inquiries weekdays between 9 A.M. and 5 P.M., EST.

Commodity Futures Trading Commission
Office of Proceedings
2033 K Street NW
Washington, DC 20581
202-254-3067

If you're interested in finding out about gold, silver, copper, and aluminum futures and about options on gold and silver futures, call the Commodity Exchange at the number listed below any weekday between 9 A.M. and 5 P.M., EST. Brochures detailing the intricacies of commodity trading as well as a list of COMEX member firms can be obtained by dialing **212-938-2900** during the same hours.

Commodity Exchange, Inc. (COMEX)
4 World Trade Center
New York, NY 10048
212-938-2935

○ Credit   See *Business: Credit Unions.*

○ Family Economics

The Family Economics Research Group is a government-sponsored research center that will provide you with information about the economic aspects of family living, family resources, budgets, food bills, clothing bills, insurance, and child costs. Tips about efficient management of money and time are also available. Call any weekday between 7:30 A.M. and 4:30 P.M., EST.

Family Economics Research Group
ARF, NER
6505 Belcrest Road
Federal Building, Room 442A
Hyattsville, MD 20782
301-436-8461

o Financial Planning

If you're uncomfortable with the new tax laws and concerned about saving or investing to secure your financial future, call the Institute of Certified Financial Planners (ICFP). One of their many certified financial planners can give you an overview of what this new profession is about and provide you with a list of members in your area who can spell out details. The telephone is answered weekdays between 8:30 A.M. and 5 P.M., MST.

Institute of Certified Financial Planners (ICFP)
3443 S. Galena, Suite 190
Denver, CO 80231
303-751-7600

If you're absolutely confounded every time you try to logically and creatively plan for your financial future, the International Association for Financial Planning (IAFP) may be able to help by putting you in touch with a specially trained financial planner. Upon request, IAFP will also mail you a list of member practitioners working in your area and a copy of the booklet *Building a Capital Base: A Guide to Personal Financial Planning.* A member will answer your inquiries weekdays between the hours of 9 A.M. and 5 P.M., EST.

International Association for Financial
    Planning (IAFP)
5775 Peachtree Dunwoody Road NE
Atlanta, GA 30342
404-252-9600
800-241-2148 (For booklet only)

○ **Funeral Costs** See *Death and Dying: Funeral Arrangements.*

○ Futures and Options

MercLine is a computerized system that contains up-to-the-minute data on the Chicago Mercantile Exchange (CME) contracts and markets. Callers can obtain futures and options updates as well as information of general interest on the exchange and the world economy. Because MercLine uses a multiline disk system to answer calls, updates can be made while the equipment is in use. Information contained on the MercLine is compiled by the CME Statistics Department and is furnished without responsibility for accuracy. Calls are accepted 24 hours a day, every day of the week.

MercLine
Chicago Mercantile Exchange
Statistics Department
30 S. Wacker Drive
Chicago, IL 60606
312-930-8282

○ Income Taxes

If you need help with your federal tax forms, the IRS would be happy to help you. To find the number of the IRS information center nearest you, dial **800-555-1212** and tell the operator where you're calling from. He or she will have the number for you in a second.

IRS
Taxpayer Service Division
1111 Constitution Avenue NW
Washington, DC 20224
800-555-1212

○ Insurance

If you're having trouble figuring out whether the car insurance policy that your sister recommends is the best one for you or whether the home insurance policy that your neighbor recommends will provide you with adequate coverage, call the Insurance Information Institute. Although the institute cannot provide you with detailed information about individual policies, it can provide you with general information about assessing various property and casualty insurance policies. If you desire, it can also refer you to sources of more detailed information. The line is open on weekdays from 9 A.M. to 5 P.M., EST.

Insurance Information Institute
110 William Street
New York, NY 10038
800-221-4954

The staff at the American Council of Life Insurance will try to provide at least a general answer to any question you might have regarding life insurance. If a staff member can't provide you with satisfactory information, you'll be referred to a specialist who can. Complaints about insurance brokers and policies are also accepted here. Call on a weekday anytime between 9 A.M. and 5 P.M., EST.

American Council of Life Insurance
Information Services
1850 K Street NW
Washington, DC 20006
800-423-8000
202-862-4000 (In Washington, DC)

○ Investment Clubs

If you're interested in forming an investment club, the National Association of Investors Corp. will probably be able to tell you the most expeditious way of going about it. It can also provide information on how to invest and what to invest in. A packet of information spelling out details is available upon request. Calls are accepted weekdays between 9 A.M. and 5 P.M., CST.

National Association of Investors Corp.
P.O. Box 220
Royal Oak, MI 48068
313-543-0612

○ **Personal Property Appraisals**   (See also *Home Maintenance: Real Estate Appraisals.*)

The Appraisers Association of America will provide you with a list of real estate and personal property appraisers (with their area of expertise) working in your area of the country. The association can also supply you with the names of appraisers working in some parts of Europe and Canada. Call weekdays between 9 A.M. and 5 P.M., EST.

Appraisers Association of America
60 E. 42d Street
New York, NY 10165
212-867-9775

○ **Stocks**

For a flat 50-cent charge nationwide, the Dow Jones Wall Street Closing Report information line will give you a daily update of the major gainers and losers on the stock market. The line is open weekdays, 24 hours a day.

Dow Jones Wall Street Closing Report
900-976-4141

Believe it or not, a member of the American Stock Exchange will take time out from the daily bedlam of Wall Street to answer general questions about the rules, regulations, and interpretation of same that guide the trading of stocks on that exchange. The member who answers will also refer you to an arbitration board if you would like to lodge a complaint. Call weekdays from 9 A.M. to 5 P.M., EST.

American Stock Exchange
Rulings and Inquiries Department
86 Trinity Place
New York, NY 10006
212-306-1450

If you're considering legal action against a stockbroker, contact the New York City office of the National Association of Securities Dealers (NASD) listed below. The association is in charge of arbitration and will tell you how to go about taking action. For other queries and complaints, dial the district office nearest you. The offices are open on weekdays during regular business hours.

National Association of
  Securities Dealers, Inc.
Arbitration Department
2 World Trade Center, 98th
  Floor
New York, NY 10048
212-839-6244

National Association of
  Securities Dealers, Inc.
National Headquarters
1735 K Street NW
Washington, DC 20006
202-728-8000

NASDAQ Data Center
80 Merritt Boulevard
Trumbull, CT 06611
203-385-4500

NASD District Offices
District 1
1 Union Square, Suite 1911
Seattle, WA 98101
206-624-0790

District 2N
425 California Street, Room
  1400
San Francisco, CA 94101
415-781-3434

District 2S
727 W. 7th Street
Los Angeles, CA 90017
213-627-2122

District 3
1401 17th Street, Suite 700
Denver, CO 80202
303-298-7234

District 4
911 Main Street, Suite 2230
Kansas City, MO 64105
816-421-5700

District 5
1004 Richards Building
New Orleans, LA 70112
504-522-6527

District 6
1999 Bryan Street
Olympia and York Tower,
   Suite 1450
Dallas, TX 75201
214-969-7050

District 7
250 Piedmont Avenue NE
Atlanta, GA 30308
404-658-9191

District 8
3 First National Plaza, Suite
   1680
Chicago, IL 60602
312-236-7222

District 9
1940 E. 6th Street, 5th Floor
Cleveland, OH 44114
216-694-4545

District 10
1125 15th Street NW
Washington, DC 20006
202-728-3145

District 11
1818 Market Street, 12th
   Floor
Philadelphia, PA 19103
215-665-1180

District 12
2 World Trade Center
South Tower, 98th Floor
New York, NY 10048
212-839-6200

District 13
50 Milk Street
Boston, MA 02109
617-482-0466

○ U.S. Savings Bonds

The U.S. Department of the Treasury's Bureau of Public Debt
(an ever-expanding division, I'm sure) will provide callers with
general information about U.S. savings bonds and will answer
any questions you might have about lost, stolen, or mutilated

bonds, reissuing and redemption, the going rate for bonds, and receipt (or lack thereof) of interest. The telephone is answered on weekdays between 9 A.M. and 5 P.M., EST.

U.S. Department of the Treasury
Bureau of Public Debt
P.O. Box 1328
Parkersburg, WV 26106–1328
304-420-6112

• PET CARE

Say your cat is acting peculiarly—you may be able to get instant advice from the staff at the U.S. Department of Agriculture's Extension Service. The trained staff will help you diagnose the animal's ailment and will suggest remedies. By the way, the staff is prepared to answer questions concerning the diseases and cures of both house pets and farm animals. Calls are taken weekdays from 7:30 A.M. to 4:30 P.M., EST.

U.S. Department of Agriculture
Extension Service
South Building, Room 3334
Washington, DC 20250
202-447-2677

• POISON CONTROL CENTERS

If you fear that you, your child, or a friend has ingested a toxic substance, the first thing to do is *not* to panic. Second, call the local poison control center (listed by state below). A trained staff member will provide you with instant information about antidotes and will advise you if treatment by a specialist is required. All lines are answered 24 hours a day, year round.

Alabama	800-462-0800
Alaska	907-563-3393 (Call collect)
Arizona	800-362-0101
Arkansas	501-661-6161 (Call collect)
California	916-453-3692 (Sacramento residents)
	800-852-7221 (Central California)
	619-294-6000 (Southern California)
	415-666-2845 (Northern California)
Colorado	303-629-1123 (Denver)
	800-332-3073 (Statewide)
Connecticut	203-674-3456 (Call collect)
Delaware	302-655-3389
District of Columbia	202-625-3333 (Call collect)
Florida	800-342-3222
Georgia	800-282-5846
Guam	671-646-5801 or
	671-646-8104
Hawaii	808-941-4411 (Honolulu)
	800-362-3585
Idaho	800-632-8000
Illinois	800-252-2022
Indiana	800-382-9097
Iowa	800-272-6477
Kansas	800-332-6633
Kentucky	800-722-5725
Louisiana	318-425-1524 (Shreveport)
	800-535-0525
Maine	207-871-2381 (Portland)
	800-442-6305
Maryland	301-528-7701 (Baltimore)
	800-492-2414
Massachusetts	617-232-2120 (Boston)
	800-682-9211
Michigan	313-494-5711 (Detroit)
	800-572-1655
	800-462-6642

Minnesota	**612-221-2113** (St. Paul)
	800-222-1222
Mississippi	**601-354-7660**
Missouri	**800-392-9111**
Montana	**800-525-5042**
Nebraska	**800-642-9999**
Nevada	**702-789-3013** or
	702-785-4129
New Hampshire	**603-646-5000** (Hanover)
	800-562-8236
New Jersey	**800-962-1253**
New Mexico	**505-843-2551** (Albuquerque)
	800-432-6866
New York	**607-723-8929** (Binghamton region)
	716-878-7654 (Buffalo region)
	518-792-3151 (Glens Falls region)
	212-340-4494 (New York City region)
	716-275-5151 (Rochester region)
	518-382-4039 (Schenectady region)
	315-476-7529 (Syracuse region)
North Carolina	**800-672-1697**
North Dakota	**701-280-5575** (Fargo)
	800-732-2200
Ohio	**800-362-9922**
Oklahoma	**405-271-5454** (Oklahoma City)
	800-522-4611
Oregon	**503-225-8968** (Portland)
	800-452-7165
Pennsylvania	Call emergency room at local hospital.
Rhode Island	**401-277-5727** (Call collect)
South Carolina	**803-765-7359** (Columbia)
	800-922-1117
South Dakota	**605-336-3894** (Sioux Falls)
	800-952-0123
Tennessee	**615-322-6435**
Texas	**800-392-8548**
Utah	**801-581-2151** (Salt Lake)
	800-662-0062
Vermont	**802-658-3456** (Call collect)

Virginia	804-924-5543 (Western half of state; call collect)
	804-786-9123 (Eastern half of state; call collect)
Washington	206-526-2121 (Seattle)
	800-732-6985
	509-747-1077 (Spokane)
	800-572-5842
West Virginia	304-348-4211 (Charleston)
	800-642-3625
Wisconsin	608-262-3702 (Call collect)
	414-931-4114 (Call collect)
Wyoming	307-635-9256 (Cheyenne)
	800-442-2704

• POSTAL SERVICE

o Complaints

If you have a complaint about any aspect of your postal service, call your local post office. If your problem is not adequately resolved, call the Office of Consumer Affairs at the U.S. Postal Service. The office will investigate and help seek a solution. The staff also provides information on specific products and services. The office is open every weekday between 7:30 A.M. and 5 P.M., EST.

U.S. Postal Service
Office of Consumer Affairs
475 L'Enfant Plaza SW
Washington, DC 20260
202-245-4514

o Philately See *Collectibles: Stamps.*

o Rates, Fees, and Zip Codes

Need to know the zip code for Walla Walla, Washington? Call your local post office. A postal worker will give you all the information you need about postal rates, fees, and zip codes. If by chance nobody there can help you, call the U.S. Post Office weekdays from 8 A.M. to 8 P.M., EST, and Saturdays from 8 A.M. to 5 P.M.

U.S. Post Office
2 Massachusetts Avenue NE
Washington, DC 20066
202-682-9595

• PREGNANCY, BIRTHING, AND FAMILY PLANNING (See also *Children and Child Care.*)

○ General Information (See also *Information Centers: Women.*)

The Katharine Dexter McCormick Library of the Planned Parenthood Federation of America was established two decades ago to help both the lay and professional communities to pursue their informational or research needs in the field of family planning and sexuality education. A partial listing of their specialized collections includes contraception and contraceptive research, human sexuality, Margaret Sanger, patient education, reproductive education, sociopolitical aspects of sexuality, teenage sexuality, and women's status. If you have a question pertaining to any area of family planning and sexuality, try the library of your local chapter of Planned Parenthood first. If they haven't the resources to provide you with a satisfactory answer, dial the national headquarters at the number listed below. Your inquiries will be fielded weekdays from 9:30 A.M. to 4:30 P.M., EST.

Planned Parenthood Federation, Inc.
810 Seventh Avenue
New York, NY 10019
212-603-4637

○ **Abortion** (See also *Health: Women's Health Network.*)

One of the goals of the National Abortion Federation is to disseminate accurate information to consumers, legislators, and medical professionals about abortion and reproductive health. Women and men are encouraged to call to get straight answers to their questions about pregnancy, abortion, clinics, costs, insurance coverage, parental consent, legal action perhaps affecting access to abortion, or any other issue pertaining to abortion and reproduction. You are also welcome to complain about a particular physician or facility at this number; the NAF will see that investigative action is taken. NAF's free and readily comprehensible booklet, *The Consumer's Guide to Abortion Services*, written in both Spanish and English, offers information about the abortion procedure, fees, medication, follow-up care, counseling, and birth control and will be sent to you upon request. Call any weekday between 9:30 A.M. and 5:30 P.M., EST.

NAF Consumer Hotline
National Abortion Federation
900 Pennsylvania Avenue SE
Washington, DC 20003
800-772-9100

○ **Cesareans and VBACs**

Cesareans/Support, Education and Concern (C/SEC) wants to inform women and men about cesareans and to humanize medical attitudes and policies. As such, C/SEC will provide information and support to both parents and professionals regarding cesarean childbirth, cesarean prevention, and VBACs (vaginal births after cesareans). Over-the-phone counseling is available as is a list of regional support groups. Call any weekday between 9 A.M. and 5 P.M., EST; after hours, leave a message on the answering machine. Someone will return your call shortly.

Cesareans/Support, Education and Concern
(C/SEC)
22 Forest Road
Framingham, MA 01701
617-877-8266

○ Family Planning

The National Clearinghouse for Family Planning Information document collection covers the following topics (among others): contraception and contraceptive methods; teenage pregnancy and parenthood; reproductive health; examination procedures; sexuality education; menstruation, menopause, and human reproduction; legal aspects of family planning; infertility; male role in family planning; population concerns; family planning for disabled persons; sterilization; sexually transmitted diseases; health education techniques; and motivation in family planning. Publications (many in Spanish) are also available as are referrals if necessary to other information centers. Counseling is not available. Call any weekday between 8:30 A.M. and 5 P.M., EST.

National Clearinghouse for Family Planning
  Information
Health and Human Services Department
P.O. Box 12921
Arlington, VA 22209
703-558-7932

○ Father-Coached Childbirth

The American Academy of Husband-Coached Childbirth was founded by Robert A. Bradley and Marjie and Jay Hathaway for the purpose of making childbirth education information available. The academy teaches only the Bradley method, the principles of which include active participation of the father as coach, excellent nutrition, avoidance of drugs, relaxation, breast-feeding beginning at birth, and parent responsibility. If you would like more information on the Bradley method or would like to know if you qualify to be a Bradley instructor, call the national office any weekday between 8:30 A.M. and 2:30 P.M., PST. Referrals to local Bradley method instructors are also available.

American Academy of Husband-Coached
  Childbirth
P.O. Box 5224
Sherman Oaks, CA 91413–5224
800-423-2397

○ Home Pregnancy Tests

Registered nurses on call at this division of Advanced Care Products Corp. will discuss contents and administration of three self-administered pregnancy tests and of a relief product for menstrual discomfort. Product literature is also available. Call weekdays between 8 A.M. and 3 P.M., EST.

Advanced Care Products Corp.
Ortho Pharmaceuticals
Route 202
Raritan, NJ 08869
800-526-3979
800-942-7766 (In New Jersey)

○ Infertility   See *Health: Infertility*

○ Lesbian Mothers

Lesbian Mothers' National Defense Fund (LMNDF) is a volunteer organization designed to meet the needs of lesbian women facing child custody and visitation battles in which their lesbianism is, or may become, an issue. To this end, LMNDF provides information—including personal and emotional support, prelegal advice, referrals, alternative conception and adoption information, and the names of speakers and titles of films for educational purposes—to judges, attorneys, caseworkers, and parents. The staff also has access to a large resource file of literature and case law. The phone is answered 24 hours by a service; leave a message and someone will return your call shortly.

Lesbian Mothers' National Defense Fund
P.O. Box 21567
Seattle, WA 98111
206-325-2643

○ **Maternal Health** (See also *Health: Women's Health Network.*)

Culling from 2000 volumes, the midwives and child-care professionals at the Maternity Center Association will provide callers with general information about maternal health, preparation for childbearing, midwifery, birth, infant care, and improvements in maternity care. Calls are taken on weekdays from noon until 1 P.M. and from 7 P.M. to 8 P.M., EST.

Maternity Center Association
48 E. 92d Street
New York, NY 10128
212-369-7300

○ **Midwifery**

If you're interested in turning in your present scraggly old physician for a qualified midwife, the staff at the American College of Nurse-Midwives will provide you with the name and address of one in your area. Information on educational programs for midwives is also available at this number. Call any weekday between 8:30 A.M. and 5 P.M., EST.

American College of Nurse-Midwives
1522 K Street NW
Suite 1120
Washington, DC 20005
202-347-5445

○ **Nutrition**   See *Children and Child Care: Nutrition.*

○ Preparation for Childbirth

The American Society for Psychoprophylaxis in Obstetrics/ Lamaze (ASPO/Lamaze), an education, advocacy, and support organization composed of childbirth educators, public health nurses, physical therapists, nurse-midwives, psychologists, maternal and child health nurses, and other health professionals, is committed to family-centered maternity care. When you call, a staff member can provide you with information on the Lamaze method of childbirth and on continuing education workshops. If you would like the name and number of the nearest Lamaze instructor in your area, dial **800-368-4404,** any weekday between 9 A.M. and 5 P.M., EST. For general information, call the office listed below. Someone will help you weekdays between 9 A.M. and 5 P.M., EST.

American Society for Psychoprophylaxis in
  Obstetrics/Lamaze
1840 Wilson Boulevard
Suite 204
Arlington, VA 22201
800-368-4404

○ Toxic Substances and Birth Defects

If you're concerned about the danger presented by toxic substances or radiation exposure to you or your infant, the National Network to Prevent Birth Defects (NNPBD) is the first place to seek answers. The center has studies underway on the effects of certain toxic substances on male infertility, chlorinated and brominated chemicals in breast milk, so-called therapeutic drugs during pregnancy, and exposure to heavy metals in the workplace and fallout from commercial nuclear plants. General information is free; a copy charge is billed for reprints of articles and studies. The line is answered by a person or a machine 24 hours a day; if you get the machine, leave a message and someone will get back to you shortly.

National Network to Prevent Birth Defects
  (NNPBD)
P.O. Box 15309
South East Station
Washington, DC 20003
202-543-5450

• PRESIDENT'S DAILY SCHEDULE

For what it's worth, this prerecorded message, changed every morning, will give you the details of the President's daily schedule. Call anytime.

President's Daily Schedule
Office of the Press Secretary
The White House
Washington, DC 20500
202-456-2343

R

• RAPE

○ Child Sexual Abuse See *Children and Child Care: Sexual Abuse.*

○ Emergency Services

Fern Ferguson, president of the National Coalition against Sexual Assault (NCASA), suggests that victims of rape or sexual assault follow these safety tips:

1. Ensure your immediate safety.
2. Get medical attention as soon as possible; it is important physically and emotionally, even if you have no obvious injuries. A medical exam should include a pelvic exam (or a rectal exam if you were raped anally), treatment of any external injuries, treatment for the prevention of sexually transmitted disease, and treatment for the prevention of pregnancy. Don't hesitate to ask a friend or counselor from the local rape crisis counseling center to go to the hospital with you.
3. Report the rape to the police. If you do not want to prosecute, in many states, you may report anonymously.
4. Ensure your long-term safety. This means emotional and physical. You may desire some counseling. Most rape crisis centers offer support and counseling; you can find the center nearest you by checking your local phone directory under "Rape Crisis" or "Sexual Assault Counseling." If you can't find a listing under these headings, call a local hospital or women's center. If you are still unsuccessful, call either the state coalition (see Domestic Violence Hotlines), the regional representative of NCASA, or the president of NCASA.

The regional representatives' and the president's numbers are listed below. The telephones are answered during normal business hours for the area.

NCASA Region I
Tina Utley Edwards
YWCA Rape Crisis Service of
  Greater Utica
1000 Cornelia Street
Utica, NY 13502
315-797-7740

NCASA Region II
Brenda Robinson
Anne Arundel County
Sexual Offense Crisis Center
62 Cathedral Street
Annapolis, MD 21401
301-224-1321

NCASA Region III
Nancy Beile
Sexual Violence Program
1222 W. 31st Street
Minneapolis, MN 55408
612-824-2864

NCASA Region IV
Peg Ziegler
Rape Crisis Center
80 Butler Street SE
Atlanta, GA 30335
404-588-4861

NCASA Region V
Anne Byrne
Rape Assistance and
  Awareness
Box 112
640 Broadway
Denver, CO 80203
303-329-9922

NCASA Region VI
Carolyn Byerly
127 North Bowdoin Place
Seattle, WA 98103
206-634-3652

NCASA President
Fern Y. Ferguson
Volunteers of America
8787 State Street, Suite 202
East St. Louis, IL 62203
618-398-7764

O Marital and Date Rape (See also *Domestic Violence Hotlines.*)

The staff of the National Clearinghouse on Marital and Date Rape (NCOMR) provides callers with the latest data on court cases, recent and pending legislation on the issue, and information on the social, political, legal, economic, religious, and philosophical history of the attitudes supporting the exemption from prosecution of husbands and dates who rape their wives and lovers. NCOMR provides a referral service to researchers and reporters seeking marital-rape survivors for interviews and to prosecutors seeking other prosecutors, social workers, and psychologists to use as expert witnesses. NCOMR has a roster of speakers and holds training programs and seminars with the media. Battered women's shelters, rape crisis centers, clergy, and counselors are encouraged to call for advice, technical assistance, and referrals. Detailed information, strategy, library search, etc., are available on an annual sliding-fee scale. (The fee covers access to the network and library of 1000 files of briefs, statutes, articles, fact sheets, testimony, and videotapes). There is a $5 charge for each 15 minutes of staff time. Inquiries are accepted on weekdays during regular business hours, PST.

National Clearinghouse on Marital and Date
  Rape
2325 Oak Street
Berkeley, CA 94708
415-548-1770

○ **Sexual Harassment**   See *Business: Sexual Harassment.*

• READING AND WRITING

○ Book Search

If you're looking for a book but can't find it anywhere, call the Readers Express. Via a computerized search system, the Readers Express will locate any book in print and mail it to you within a few days for the cost of the book plus $2. Payment can be made by credit card only; however, gift wrapping is free. Call any weekday between 8 A.M. and 11 P.M., EST.

Readers Express
104 Fifth Avenue
New York, NY 10011
800-852-5000

○ Books for the Blind and Physically Handicapped

The National Library Service for the Blind and Physically Handicapped is a free national library program of braille and recorded materials for the blind and physically handicapped persons; it makes available over 41,000 titles—including mysteries, novels, how-to guides, science fiction, political science, biographies, best-sellers, and children's books—to its patrons. Reading materials are distributed to a cooperating network of 56 regional and over 100 local libraries, where they are circulated to eligible borrowers. Reading materials and playback machines are sent to borrowers and returned to the libraries by postage-free mail. A limited number of titles are produced in Spanish and some other languages. Seventy magazines on disc and braille are also offered; readers may request free subscriptions to *U.S. News and World Report, National Geographic, Consumer Reports,* and *Jack and Jill,* among others. A collection of over 30,000 musical items is also available. For more information about the Talking Books program and to find out whether you are eligible, contact your local librarian or leave your name and address on the answering machine at the number listed below. Information will be mailed to you within two weeks.

National Library Service for the
  Blind and Physically Handicapped
Library of Congress
Washington, DC 20542
800-424-9100

○ Copyright Information

If you need information about the copyright law or about procedures for making registration and securing a copyright on personal, creative work, call the number listed below. Someone will be happy to answer your questions weekdays between 8:30 A.M. and 5 P.M., EST. If you're already familiar with the procedure and simply need to order the appropriate forms, dial the Copyright Forms Hotline at **202-287-9100.** Your order will be taken 24 hours a day, seven days a week.

Copyright Public Information Office
101 Independence Avenue SE
Washington, DC 20559
202-287-8700

○ Grammar and Writing Hotlines

Dangling modifiers got you down? Call your nearest grammar hotline. A trained grammarian will not only tell you how to secure your modifier but also answer any other question you have about grammar, punctuation, spelling, capitalization, and usage. Rumor has it that the staff has yet to be stumped. Because most writing hotlines are sponsored by colleges and universities, they often reduce their hours during the summer and close during college breaks. The following hotlines are arranged alphabetically by state, except for Canada which follows the U.S. listings.

Writing Center Hotline
Auburn University
Auburn, AL 36830
(9 A.M. to noon, 1 P.M. to 4
   P.M., EST, Monday
   through Thursday; 9 A.M.
   to noon, Friday)
205-826-5749

The Writer's Hotline
University of Arkansas at
   Little Rock
Little Rock, AR 72204
(8 A.M. to noon, CST,
   weekdays) **501-569-3162**

Grammar Hotline
Moorpark College
Moorpark, CA 93021
(8 A.M. to noon, PST,
  weekdays) **805-529-2321**

U.S.C. Grammar Hotline
University of Southern
  Colorado
Pueblo, CO 81001
(9:30 A.M. to 3:30 P.M., MST,
  weekdays) **303-549-2787**

Grammar Hotline
University School of Nova
  University
Ft. Lauderdale, FL 33314
(8 A.M. to 4 P.M., EST,
  Monday through
  Thursday; 8 A.M. to 2 P.M.,
  Friday) **305-475-7697**

Grammar Hotline
Eastern Illinois University
Charleston, IL 61920
(10 A.M. to 3 P.M., CST,
  weekdays; noon to 3 P.M.,
  usual summer hours)
  217-581-5929

Grammar Hotline
Illinois State University
Normal, IL 61761
(8 A.M. to 4:30 P.M., CST,
  weekdays) **309-438-2345**

Grammarphone
Triton College
River Grove, IL 60171
(8:30 A.M. to 9 P.M., CST,
  Monday through
  Thursday; 8:30 A.M. to 5
  P.M., Friday; 10 A.M. to 1
  P.M., Saturday)
  312-456-0300, ext. **254**

Grammar Hotline
Purdue University
West Lafayette, IN 47907
(9:30 A.M. to 3 P.M., EST;
  closed late April through
  mid-June and all of
  August) **317-494-3723**

Writer's Hotline
Emporia State University
Emporia, KS 66801
(11:30 A.M. to 4:30 P.M., CST,
  Monday through
  Thursday; 7 P.M. to 9:30
  P.M., Thursday nights
  during the spring and fall
  semesters) **316-343-1200**,
  ext. **380**

Grammarphone
Frostburg State College
Frostburg, MD 21532
(10 A.M. to noon, EST,
  weekdays) **301-689-4327**
  (Call collect)

Grammar Hotline
Northeastern University
Boston, MA 02115
(8:30 A.M. to 4:30 P.M., EST,
  weekdays) **617-437-2512**

Writer's Hotline
University of Missouri at
  Kansas City
Kansas City, MO 64110–
  2499
(9 A.M. to 4 P.M., CST,
  weekdays, September
  through May; summer
  hours from 1 June through
  16 July) **816-276-2244**

Grammar Hotline
Missouri Southern State
  College
Joplin, MO 64801
(9 A.M. to 2 P.M., CST,
  weekdays; closed from 15
  May to 25 August)
  417-624-0171

Rewrite
York College of the City
  University of New York
Jamaica, NY 11451
(1 P.M. to 4 P.M., EST,
  weekdays) **212-739-7483**

Dial-A-Grammar
Raymond Walters College
Cincinnati, OH 45236
513-745-4312
Tapes requests; will return
call with answer (long-
distance calls returned
collect)

Writer's Remedies
University of Cincinnati
Cincinnati, OH 45221
(Noon to 1 P.M. and 2 P.M.
  to 3 P.M., EST, Monday,
  Wednesday, Thursday,
  and Friday) **513-475-2493**

Writing Center Hotline
Cincinnati Technical
  College
Cincinnati, OH 45223
(9 A.M. to 4:15 P.M., EST,
  weekdays) **513-559-1520**

Writing Resource Center
Ohio Wesleyan University
Delaware, OH 43015
(9 A.M. to noon and 1 P.M.
  to 4 P.M., EST, weekdays)
  614-369-4431, ext. **301**

Academic Support Center
Writing Center Hotline
Cedar Crest College
Allentown, PA 18104
(9 A.M. to 4 P.M., EST,
  weekdays, September
  through May)
  215-437-4471

Grammar Hotline
Lincoln University
Lincoln University, PA
  19352
(8 A.M. to 5 P.M., EST,
  weekdays, fall semester; 9
  A.M. to 5 P.M., EST,
  weekdays, spring
  semester; summer hours
  vary) **215-932-8300**, ext.
  460

Writer's Hotline
University of South Carolina
Columbia, SC 29208
(8:30 A.M. to 5 P.M., EST,
    Monday through
    Thursday; 8:30 A.M. to 1
    P.M., Friday) **803-777-7020**

Learning Line
San Antonio College
San Antonio, TX 78284
(8 A.M. to 9:45 P.M., CST,
    Monday through
    Thursday; 8 A.M. to 4 P.M.,
    Friday) **512-733-2503**

Grammar Hotline
Tidewater Community
    College
Virginia Beach, VA 23456
(10 A.M. to 12:30 P.M. and
    1:30 P.M. to 2 P.M., EST,
    Monday through
    Thursday; 10 A.M. to noon,
    EST, reduced hours in
    summer) **804-427-7170**

Grammar Hotline
Grant MacEwan
    Community College
Edmonton
Alberta, Canada T5J2P2
(10 A.M. to 2 P.M., MST,
    weekdays) **403-483-4393**

Grammar Hotline
University of New
    Brunswick
Fredericton
New Brunswick, Canada
    E3B5A3
(Variable hours)
    506-453-4666

● **RECREATION** See *Outdoors and Recreation.*

● **RUNAWAYS** See *Children and Child Care: Runaways.*

S

• SELF-HELP GROUPS

Self-help groups consist of people who share a common experience and wish to assist each other without the use of a trained professional (such as a psychiatrist or social worker). Such groups have proliferated in the United States during the past ten years; recent estimates put the total number of groups across the country at over 500,000. Although many concern themselves with various health issues, others have been formed by people who share a common situation; for example, there's a self-help group for nurses, one for female filmmakers, and a third for Soviet Jewish immigrants. To find out if there's a group near you concerned with what's of concern to you, call the National Self-Help Clearinghouse at the number listed below. If there is no group in your area and you'd like to start one, the staff can provide you with information on starting a group. Publications and hints about what to look for in a group you're considering joining are also available. The office is open every weekday from 10 A.M. to 5 P.M., EST.

National Self-Help Clearinghouse
Graduate School and University Center
City University of New York
33 W. 42d Street, Room 1227
New York, NY 10036
212-840-1259

• SEXUAL ABUSE

O **Children**   See *Children and Child Care: Sexual Abuse.*
O **Domestic**   See *Domestic Violence Hotlines.*

○ **Harassment** See *Business: Sexual Harassment.*

○ **Rape** See *Rape.*

● **SINGLE PARENTS** See *Children and Child Care: Single Parents.*

● **SKIN CARE** See *Hair and Skin Care: Skin.*

● **SMOKING** See *Civil Rights: Nonsmokers' Rights; Health: Smoking.*

● **SPACE EXPLORATION** See *Aeronautics and Space Exploration.*

● **SPORTS AND ATHLETICS**

○ **General Information**

The staff of the National Library of Sports will answer any general question you have about sports and athletics. The library contains over 150,000 items, including old guides to most sports and biographies of athletes and events. It is open weekdays from 1 P.M. to 5 P.M., PST.

National Library of Sports
San Jose Public Library
180 W. San Carlos Street
San Jose, CA 95113
408-287-0993

○ **Baseball** (See also *Collectibles: Baseball Cards.*)

The reference librarian at the National Baseball Library (part of the National Baseball Hall of Fame) will provide you with answers to any general questions you have about the history of baseball, the players, or the game. Among other things, the library contains the official records of the major leagues. The reference desk answers inquiries weekdays between 9 A.M. and 5 P.M., EST.

National Baseball Library
Cooperstown, NY 13326
607-547-9988

○ **Basketball**

If you've been arguing a fine point of basketball etiquette with a friend for two weeks, you can settle the dispute by calling the experts at the Naismith Memorial Basketball Library. The library contains, among other notable items, copies of all the rule books and guides to basketball ever published, minutes of the meetings of the National Association of Basketball Coaches, and thousands of yearbooks and press guides. The librarian also has access to a complete picture file. The library is open every weekday from 9 A.M. to 5 P.M., EST.

Naismith Memorial Basketball Library
1150 W. Columbus
Springfield, MA 01101–0179
413-781-6500

○ **Fly Fishing**

The reference librarian at the Museum of American Fly Fishing, Inc., Library will provide you with answers to any questions you have about fly fishing or its history, fish lore, angling, and entomology. Call any time between 10 A.M. and 4 P.M., EST, seven days a week.

Museum of American Fly Fishing, Inc., Library
Manchester, VT 05254
802-362-3300

○ Football

If you've got a question about pro football, call Joe Horrigan, the curator, or Ann Mangus, the librarian, at the Pro Football Hall of Fame Library and Research Center. This singular information center contains copies of all the Spalding football guides (1892–1940) as well as pre-NFL rare documents. The center is open every weekday from 9 A.M. to 5 P.M., EST.

Pro Football Hall of Fame Library and
   Research Center
2121 George Hallas Drive
Canton, OH 44708
216-456-8207

○ Golf

If you have any question about golf—its history, rules, or state of the art today—the U.S. Golf Association's library, which contains 7000 books, 440 bound periodicals, and 35 books of newspaper clippings, is the first place to turn. The reference librarian will be happy to help you weekdays between 8:30 A.M. and 5 P.M., EST, and from 10 A.M. to 4 P.M. on Saturdays and Sundays.

U.S. Golf Association
Golf House Library
Far Hills, NJ 07931
201-234-2300

○ Hockey

What are the dimensions of an official hockey puck? Call the U.S. Hockey Hall of Fame Library and find out. The research librarian has access to hundreds of periodicals, programs, press guides, and books and will be happy to help you during the following hours:

From Labor Day to 14 June:	9 A.M. to 5 P.M., CST, Monday through Saturday; noon to 5 P.M., CST, Sunday
From 15 June to Labor Day:	9 A.M. to 8 P.M., CST, Monday through Saturday; 10 A.M. to 8 P.M., CST, Sunday

U.S. Hockey Hall of Fame
P.O. Box 657
Eveleth, MN 55734
218-744-5167

○ Physical Fitness Programs

Although the staff members at the President's Council on Physical Fitness and Sports cannot provide you with personal advice, they can give you general information about exercise, physical education programs, sports, and physical fitness regimens for youth and the elderly. Various publications are available; single copies are free, multiple copies are charged accordingly. A member of the council will take your call any weekday between 8:30 A.M. and 5 P.M., EST.

The President's Council on
  Physical Fitness and Sports
450 5th Street NW
Suite 7103
Washington, DC 20001
202-272-3430

○ Skiing

If you have a question about skiing, its history, or its protocol, call the Roland Palmedo Ski Library. The librarian has access to thousands of volumes and will be happy to help you any weekday between 10 A.M. and 4 P.M., EST, and between 1 P.M. and 4 P.M. on Saturdays and Sundays.

The National Ski Hall of Fame
Roland Palmedo Ski Library
P.O. Box 191
Ishpemig, MI 49849
906-486-9281

○ Sports Medicine

The hotline sponsored by the International Institute of Sports Science and Medicine (IISSM) provides callers with general information about common athletic injuries. Injuries are not diagnosed over the phone, but the staff of orthopedic surgeons and athletic trainers will give you the name of the nearest sports medicine clinic or specialist. The staff can also offer information on the field of sports medicine in general and on educational programs in sports medicine. The phone is answered every weekday between 8:30 A.M. and 4:30 P.M., CST.

International Institute of
   Sports Science and Medicine
1815 N. Capital, Suite 214
Indianapolis, IN 46202
317-926-1339
800-23-SPORT (In Indiana)

○ Sports Phone

This 24-hour service which is updated sixty times a day will provide you with all the information you need about the day's action in professional and major collegiate sports (including track and field) and will highlight, when relevant, all American Olympic events. By the way, Sports Phone, which was created in 1972, is the oldest dial-it program around.

Sports Phone
Phone Programs
919 Third Avenue
New York, NY 10022
212-976-1313

○ Swimming

If you'd like some information about improving your stroke, call the experts at the International Swimming Hall of Fame Library. They'll answer any question you have about the sport, its history, pool care and management, diving and water polo, swimmer's biographies, and swim officiating. The librarian will not, however, conduct in-depth research. The library is open weekdays from 10 A.M. to 3 P.M., EST.

International Swimming Hall of Fame Library
1 Hall of Fame Drive
Ft. Lauderdale, FL 33316
305-462-6536

○ Tennis

If you have any question about lawn or court tennis—its history, rules, or etiquette—call Jan Armstrong, the librarian at the Tennis Museum Library (part of the International Tennis Hall of Fame). She'll be happy to help you any weekday between 9 A.M. and 5 P.M., EST. (Answers may be delayed in July, which is the tennis tournament month.)

International Tennis Hall of
   Fame and Tennis Museum Library
Newport Casino
194 Bellevue Avenue
Newport, RI 02840
401-849-6378

○ Women's Sports Foundation

Founded by Billie Jean King and other female athletes, the Women's Sports Foundation has three primary objectives: to encourage and support the participation of women in sport and fitness activities; to provide opportunities, facilities, and training for girls and women in sport and fitness; and to educate women and the general public on the value of participating in sport and fitness activities. When you call their information and referral line, an expert will answer any question you have pertaining to women's sports, sports injuries, athletics, and sports medicine. Referrals to specially trained sports physicians and sports medicine clinics are also available. The foundation is particularly strong on instructional and athletic scholarship information. Educational guides and video rentals are also available. Sportsline is open on weekdays from 9 A.M. to 5 P.M., PST.

Sportsline
Women's Sports Foundation
195 Moulton Street
San Francisco, CA 94123
800-227-3988
415-563-6266 (In California, Alaska, and
Hawaii)

• SUICIDE EMERGENCY AID

The National Save-A-Life League is the oldest suicide prevention organization in the country (founded in 1906); it specializes in suicide prevention and crisis intervention. Referrals to helping agencies in the New York City metropolitan area are available; if you live outside of New York City and want the name of an agency in your area, the staff member can give you a number in your state to call for information. The phone is answered either by person or by machine 24 hours a day. If you receive the machine, the prerecorded message offers the telephone numbers of other sources of help, which you are encouraged to call if you desire immediate attention.

If you would like someone to call you back, leave a message; the staff tries to return calls within 24 hours.

National Save-A-Life League, Inc.
4520 Fourth Avenue, Suite MH3
Brooklyn, NY 11220
718-492-4067

● SUPPORT SERVICES FOR CHILDREN AND PARENTS   See *Children and Child Care.*

T

• TELEPHONE EQUIPMENT AND SERVICE

The staff at the Tele-Consumer Hotline will provide you with information about long-distance options and service, telephone equipment and repairs, ways to cut costs, how to read your bill, and where to get help to resolve billing problems. Residents of the following states are now served: Alaska, Arizona, Colorado, Delaware, District of Columbia, Florida, Georgia, Idaho, Kentucky, Louisiana, Maryland, Mississippi, Montana, New Jersey, New Mexico, North Carolina, Pennsylvania, South Carolina, Tennessee, Utah, Virginia, West Virginia, and Wyoming. The line is open weekdays from 9 A.M. to 5 P.M., EST.

Tele-Consumer Hotline
1536 16th Street NW
Washington, DC 20036
800-332-1124
202-483-4100

• TELEVISION

Arguing over the Beaver's real name again? Call the Television Information Office (TIO). This network-supported information service originated in 1959 to meet the needs of educators, students, government agencies, the press, librarians, and the lay public, and its trained staff will supply answers to any question you have about the medium, be it about television as a news medium, the image of women on television, or television as an educational resource. The library contains the most extensive range of information about the social, cultural, and programming aspects of television in the country. A TIO expert will answer your question any weekday between 9 A.M. and 5 P.M., EST.

Television Information Office
745 Fifth Avenue
New York, NY 10151
212-759-6800

● **TEXTILES** See *Fabrics and Textiles.*

● **TIME AND WEATHER**

○ **National Forecast**

To find out the weather forecast for the eastern cities of the United States (St. Louis to New York), dial **202-899-3244**. For the western cities (Kansas City to Los Angeles), dial **202-899-3249**. The prerecorded messages are changed daily and are available 24 hours a day.

National Weather Service
National Oceanic and Atmospheric
    Administration
Commerce Dept.
8060 13th Street
Silver Spring, MD 20910
202-899-3244 (For eastern cities)
202-899-3249 (For western cities)

○ **Time**

Some of us—procrastinators, chronic late-goers, and other happy rebels—were not too happy ten years ago when some clever sport thought to manufacture a digital clock. I don't know what we're going to do now that overeager parents, school principals, and church deacons can arm themselves with the correct time down to the billionth of a second. (Yes, I said billionth of a second.) Yet, for a mere 50 cents, you can call the nation's timekeepers in Washington, weirdos who, with compulsive regularity, consult twenty-four independent atomic clocks to keep the official clock at the U.S. Naval Observatory accurate to the billionth of a second. (I'm trying to get this through my head.) But beware all you wardens: if you're calling from a distant area, the beep may take 0.1 second to reach you. The time is given in eastern standard time.

U.S. Naval Observatory
900-410-TIME (What else?)

• TRAVEL

○ General Information

Although the International Airline Passengers Association is a membership organization, the staff will help the general public with inquiries regarding overbooking, lost luggage, and airplane safety, as time permits. A service agent will answer your call on weekdays, anytime between 9 A.M. and 5 P.M., CST.

International Airline Passengers Association
Consumer Affairs Division
P.O. Box 660074
Dallas, TX 75266–0074
214-438-8100

○ Air Passenger Complaints

If you have a complaint about any aspect of airplane travel, be it about lost luggage, bumping, or smokers, call the Consumer Affairs Division of the U.S. Department of Transportation. Experts will investigate your claim and help you file for reparations if necessary. A service agent is ready to help you any weekday between 9 A.M. and 5 P.M., EST. After hours you may leave your message on an answering machine, and an agent will return your call in the morning.

Consumer Affairs Division
U.S. Department of Transportation
400 7th Street SW, Room 10405
Washington, DC 20590
202-755-2220

o Bus and Rail Passenger Complaints

If you have any complaint about your ride on a bus or a train, call the Interstate Commerce Commission (ICC). The staff will investigate your claim and suggest ways of handling the problem in the future. This office also investigates claims regarding the shipment of household goods. The office is open weekdays from 8:30 A.M. to 5:30 P.M., EST.

Programs Branch
Interstate Commerce Commission
12th and Constitution Avenue NW
Washington, DC 20243
202-275-7844

o Complaints against Travel Suppliers

The American Society of Travel Agents will try to help disgruntled travelers with any problem they encounter while traveling or setting up travel plans. The society's speciality is, of course, travel agents, tour operators, and other travel suppliers. If your question cannot be answered by staff members, they will direct you to someone who can. Call weekdays between 9 A.M. and 5 P.M., EST.

American Society of Travel Agents
Consumer Affairs Department
4400 MacArthur Boulevard NW
Washington, DC 20007
202-965-7520

O Emergencies Abroad

The Citizens Emergency Center, an office of the State Department, handles emergency matters concerning U.S. citizens abroad, including missing persons, deaths, and financial assistance to stranded persons. This office is the one to call when a U.S. national is arrested abroad. The office is open every weekday from 8:15 A.M. to 5 P.M., EST.

State Department
Citizens Emergency Center
Main State Building
Washington, DC 20520
202-632-5225

O Nonsmokers' Complaints See *Civil Rights: Nonsmokers' Rights.*

V

● VETERANS

○ Benefits

If you need information about veterans' benefits, including GI loans, education, disability insurance compensation, medical care, dental treatment, and employment, call the local Veterans Administration office. It should be listed under "U.S. Government" in your phone book. If you are unable to locate the number, call the information operator at **800-555-1212**. He or she will give you the number of the regional office nearest you.

○ Vietnam Veterans

Vietnam Veterans of America is a nonprofit organization— the only organization devoted solely to veterans of the Vietnam War. Its staff will answer questions about Agent Orange, posttraumatic stress disorder, and legal matters pertaining to the caller's status as a veteran. Information about filing Agent Orange claims forms and referrals to local chapters (where job counseling can be had) are also available. Self-help guides will be mailed, if the caller desires. The Washington number is answered every weekday between 8:30 A.M. and 5 P.M., EST. If you dial the 800 number, an answering machine will record your message; leave your name and number and someone will return your call within two or three weeks.

Vietnam Veterans of America, Inc.
2001 S Street NW
Suite 700
Washington, DC 20009
202-332-4745
800-424-7275

• VOLUNTEERING

○ National Programs

If you're interested in volunteering but don't know how to find an organization that accepts volunteers, call your regional ACTION program information line. ACTION, the National Volunteer Agency, was established in 1971 to enable Americans to volunteer their services where needed. A regional information officer will provide you with all the information you need about volunteering for ACTION, VISTA, the Foster Grandparent Program, RSVP (Retired Senior Volunteer Program), the Senior Companion Program, NCSL (National Center for Service Learning), OVL (Office of Volunteer Liaison), OPP (Office of Policy and Planning), YVA (Young Volunteers in ACTION), and ADPP (ACTION Drug Prevention Program).

Region 1
ACTION
441 Stuart Street, 9th Floor
Boston, MA 02116
(8 A.M. to 5 P.M., EST, weekdays) **617-223-4501**

Region II
ACTION
Jacob K. Javits Federal Building
26 Federal Plaza, Suite 1611
New York, NY 10278
(8 A.M. to 5 P.M., EST, weekdays) **212-264-5716**

Region III
ACTION
U.S. Customs House
2d and Chestnut Streets
Room 108
Philadelphia, PA 19106
(8 A.M. to 5 P.M., EST, weekdays) **215-597-9972**

Region IV
ACTION
101 Marietta Street NW
Room 1003
Atlanta, GA 30323
(7 A.M. to 6 P.M., EST, weekdays) **404-221-2860**

Region V
ACTION
10 W. Jackson Boulevard, 3d Floor
Chicago, IL 60604
(8:30 A.M. to 5:30 P.M., CST, weekdays)
  312-353-5107
This ACTION office may move soon. If the number you dial is incorrect, please check the information operator for the correct one.

Region VI
ACTION
Federal Building
1100 Commerce Street, Room 6B11
Dallas, TX 75242
(8 A.M. to 4:30 P.M., CST, weekdays)
  214-767-9494

(*Note:* There is no Region VII.)

Region VIII
ACTION
1405 Curtis Street, Room 2930
Denver, CO 80202
(7 A.M. to 5 P.M., MST, weekdays) **303-844-2671**

Region IX
ACTION
211 Main Street, Room 530
San Francisco, CA 94105
(6:30 A.M. to 5:30 P.M., PST, weekdays)
  415-974-0673

Region X
ACTION
1111 Third Avenue, Suite 330
Seattle, WA 98101
(8 A.M. to 5 P.M., PST, weekdays) **206-442-4520**

○ Overseas

The Peace Corps needs volunteers to help in the following areas: community development, health and nutrition, agriculture, forestry and fisheries, business, science and math, education and special education, and engineering. Special programs are available for older Americans who wish to volunteer. For more information, call the number listed below. Calls are answered every weekday from 9 A.M. to 5 P.M., EST.

Peace Corps
806 Connecticut Avenue NW
Room P301
Washington, DC 20526
800-424-8580, ext. 293
202-254-9814 (In Washington, DC)

W

● **WRITING** See *Reading and Writing: Copyright Information;*
Reading and Writing: Grammar and Writing Hotlines.